T0319139

Cambridge Elements ≡

Elements in Corpus Linguistics

edited by
Susan Hunston
University of Birmingham

CONDUCTING SENTIMENT ANALYSIS

Lei Lei
Shanghai Jiao Tong University

Dilin Liu
The University of Alabama

CAMBRIDGE
UNIVERSITY PRESS

CAMBRIDGE
UNIVERSITY PRESS

University Printing House, Cambridge CB2 8BS, United Kingdom

One Liberty Plaza, 20th Floor, New York, NY 10006, USA

477 Williamstown Road, Port Melbourne, VIC 3207, Australia

314–321, 3rd Floor, Plot 3, Splendor Forum, Jasola District Centre,
New Delhi – 110025, India

103 Penang Road, #05–06/07, Visioncrest Commercial, Singapore 238467

Cambridge University Press is part of the University of Cambridge.

It furthers the University's mission by disseminating knowledge in the pursuit of
education, learning, and research at the highest international levels of excellence.

www.cambridge.org
Information on this title: www.cambridge.org/9781108829212
DOI: 10.1017/9781108909679

© Lei Lei and Dilin Liu 2021

First published 2021

A catalogue record for this publication is available from the British Library.

ISBN 978-1-108-82921-2 Paperback
ISSN 2632-8097 (online)
ISSN 2632-8089 (print)

Additional resources for this publication at www.cambridge.org/sentimentanalysis.

Conducting Sentiment Analysis

Elements in Corpus Linguistics

DOI: 10.1017/9781108909679
First published online: August 2021

Lei Lei
Shanghai Jiao Tong University

Dilin Liu
The University of Alabama

Author for correspondence: Dilin Liu, dliu@ua.edu

Abstract: This Element provides a basic introduction to sentiment analysis, aimed at helping students and professionals in corpus linguistics to understand what sentiment analysis is, how it is conducted, and where it can be applied. It begins with a definition of sentiment analysis and a discussion of the domains where sentiment analysis is conducted and used the most. Then, it introduces two main methods that are commonly used in sentiment analysis known as *supervised machine-learning* and *unsupervised learning (or lexicon-based)* methods, followed by a step-by-step explanation of how to perform sentiment analysis with R. The Element then provides two detailed examples or cases of sentiment and emotion analysis, with one using an unsupervised method and the other using a supervised learning method.

Keywords: corpus linguistics, lexicon-based, sentiment analysis, supervised machine-learning, unsupervised machine-learning

ISBNs: 9781108829212 (PB), 9781108909679 (OC)
ISSNs: 2632-8097 (online), 2632-8089 (print)

Contents

1 Sentiment Analysis: Background

1.1 Definition and Description of Sentiment Analysis

According to comprehensive reviews of its development and application (e.g., Feldman, 2013; Mäntylä, Graziotin & Kuutila, 2018; Zunic, Corcoran & Spasic, 2020), sentiment analysis is the process of using algorithms and computer technologies to systematically detect, extract, and classify the subjective information and affective states expressed in a text, such as opinions, attitudes, and emotions regarding a service, product, person, or topic. Subjective in nature, sentiments often appear in polarity terms (i.e., in terms of two polar opposites), such as favourable/unfavourable, good/bad, happy/unhappy, positive/negative, and pro/con, although neutral sentiment is a possibility. Given this fact, sentiment analyses, in essence, detect and extract subjective polarity in language to identify the sentiments and their strengths in words, sentences, and texts (Taboada et al., 2011, p. 268). More specifically, a given sentiment analysis identifies the subjectivity, polarity, and semantic orientation of the language regarding the thing, organization, or person that is being evaluated (D'Andrea et al., 2015; Feldman, 2013; Liu and Lei, 2018; Mäntylä et al., 2018; Zunic et al., 2020). It is necessary to note that while sentiment analysis often includes emotion analysis, the latter is a more specialized subcategory of sentiment analysis. As noted, sentiment analysis is an evaluation mainly in positive vs. negative polarity terms; in comparison, emotion analysis involves more in-depth examinations of various specific emotions, such as "anger," "anxiety," "disgust," "fear," "joy," and "sadness" (Giuntini et al. 2020; Ren & Quan, 2012). Emotion analysis is highly valuable in consumer business and healthcare.

Although sentiment analysis as a term defined here was reportedly first used by Nasukawa and Yi (2003), studies about sentiments and opinions began much earlier (D'Andrea et al., 2015; Mäntylä et al., 2018). According to Mäntylä et al.'s (2018) thorough review of the evolution of sentiment analysis, the origins of sentiment analysis were (1) public opinion studies in the early 1940s during WWII and (2) the analysis of subjectivity in a text using computational linguistic approaches in the 1990s. However, sentiment analysis as we know it today did not blossom until 2004, for, as Mäntylä et al.'s (2018, p. 16) review results show, "99% of the papers [on sentiment analysis] have been published after 2004." In other words, since the early 2000s, sentiment analysis has become a very popular research area and has been used in many different domains. This is because results from sentiment analyses may offer highly useful information for businesses, consumers, educational and healthcare institutions, government agencies, and political organizations concerning their products, services, patients' feelings and emotions, policies, and/or opinions regarding politicians and political parties respectively (Feldman, 2013; Mäntylä et al., 2018; Rambocas & Pacheco, 2018; Zhang, Gan & Jiang, 2014; Zunic et al., 2020). Another reason for the rapid growth of work in sentiment analysis is the public's increased access to the Internet and their growing use of social media (e.g., Facebook and Twitter) and other online business and social communication platforms (Rambocas & Pacheco, 2018; Pagolu et al., 2016; Zunic et al., 2020).

1.2 Sentiment Analysis vs. Appraisal, Stance, and Semantic Prosody

Based on the aforementioned definition, sentiment in sentiment analysis is quite similar in meaning to several known concepts in corpus linguistics that deal with evaluative language, such as appraisal (Martin & White, 2005), stance (Biber, 2006; Conrad & Biber, 2000), and semantic (or discourse) prosody (Sinclair, 1991, 2004). However, although these concepts are all concerned with evaluative language, their research foci, scopes, and/or analysis approaches differ from one another to various extents, thanks perhaps largely to what Hunston (2011, p. 10) calls "a variance in what kind of phenomenon 'evaluation' is taken to be."

Appraisal analysis, which originated in systemic functional linguistics, treats evaluation as the enactment of a system of meanings by speakers/writers through the use of various linguistic and discoursal resources to convey their approval or disapproval of ideas, persons, or things (Martin & White, 2005). As a result, appraisal analysis is quite broad in scope and involves intensive perusal of text by the researcher although some appraisal studies also make use of some simple corpus query and analysis tools, such as concordancing. In other words, the research method of appraisal studies is largely qualitative in nature. In comparison, stance analysis, arising from corpus linguistic research, considers evaluation to be "the expression of personal feelings and assessments" conveyed in words, phrases, and sentence structures that are frequently used to express evaluative meanings (Conrad & Biber, 2000, p. 57). Focusing on recurring evaluative linguistic items, stance analysis thus appears to have a smaller scope than appraisal. Furthermore, steeped in corpus linguistics, stance research also makes much more use of computer technology and statistics than appraisal analysis does. Of course, stance analysis also includes some close manual reading and analysis of the identified tokens (e.g., keywords in context in the form of concordance lines) to determine and classify the types of stance being expressed (e.g., epistemic, attitudinal, and modality stances) and their semantic/discoursal functions. In this sense, stance analysis also consists of both qualitative and quantitative examinations, but with the latter being more prominent.

Regarding semantic prosody, a term not as transparent as the others in the group, a definition is first in order. Semantic prosody refers to the phenomenon that certain seemingly neutral words may develop positive or negative associations through particular frequent collocations as shown in Sinclair's (1991, pp. 74–75) example of "set in," which acquires a negative meaning through its frequent collocation with negative nouns as its subjects, such as "decay sets in," "despair sets in," and "a malaise has set in." Hence, semantic prosody is a pragmatic unit of meaning that conveys or implies either an evaluation in terms of positive/negative polarity or a subtle affective feeling, such as "reluctance, frustration, or difficulty" (Hunston, 2011, p. 56). As such, semantic prosody often functions as implicit evaluation. An example of such implicit evaluation can be found in the sentence taken from Davies's (2008–) *Corpus of Contemporary American English*: "Whether the park can endure this onslaught of modernity is a hotly debated question in local cafs" where the author's wording "the onslaught of modernity" (along with the verb "endure") implies a negative assessment of modernity. Born out of corpus linguistics like stance analysis and with its close examination of words and their co-occurring items, semantic prosody analysis seems to also view evaluation as the expression of personal emotions and assessment. Yet its focus and scope are unique in that it concentrates on unit meanings in discourse. In terms of research method, semantic prosody analysis, like stance research again, involves extensive searches and analyses of keywords in context but has a heightened focus on collocations, colligations, and other co-occurring elements that display semantic preferences.

Now let us turn to sentiment analysis. As noted, because of its origin in computer science and computational linguistics, sentiment analysis uses statistical algorithms and, more recently, machine-learning algorithms, to identify, extract, and study emotional states and subjective information in texts from various fields and professions. Also, as will be explained in Section 2, although words of sentiment polarity are the focus in sentiment analysis, broad contextual information of these words, such as their co-occurring lexical and structural items, is also considered and factored into the final sentiment score of the text being analyzed. Therefore, the scope of sentiment analysis is quite wide both in content and linguistic information covered, and its methodology is almost exclusively quantitative and computer-technology based. Examples of actual texts with sentiment analysis will be given in Sections 2, 3, 4, and 5. While sentiment analysis also uses corpus data, its methods for identifying sentiments and opinions is much more automatic and involves only limited human judgment that all occurs in the form of building a sentiment lexicon or coding a small set of data for training purposes before the actual sentiment extraction. In other words, the extraction of sentiment itself is entirely automatic and there is no human analysis involved after the sentiments of a text have been extracted.

It is important to point out that these methodological differences used between semantic analysis and appraisal/semantic prosody analyses may also represent some of the differences between computational linguistics and corpus linguistics, two closely related disciplines whose main similarities and differences may be of importance and interest to the reader of this Element. Apart from both being disciplines of applied study of language, the two also are similar, but simultaneously different, in three aspects: the role of corpus data, research purposes, and methodology. In terms of the role of corpora, while both use corpus data in their research, such data appear to be the main object of study for corpus linguistics, but, for computational linguistics, corpora serve primarily as just a resource to solve various language-related problems. Concerning research purposes, whereas both have practical language-related research goals or applications, the scope of applications for computational linguistics appears to be wider than corpus linguistics because the former began as and has remained largely an "application-oriented enterprise" (Dipper, 2008, p. 77). As an application-driven discipline, computational linguistics has focused on natural language processing, understanding, and production for the purpose of developing various language processing and production programs or tools, such as automatic speech recognition, automated phone answering service, and machine translation (Dipper, 2008; Wilks, 2010). On the other hand, corpus linguistics has concentrated mostly on how language works, especially how words and other linguistic elements are used in actual communication, so as to help ensure more accurate and adequate linguistic description of language rules and usages in language textbooks/reference books as evidenced by the many corpus-based/informed dictionaries and textbooks produced in the past few decades, including the pioneering work *Collins COBUILD English dictionary* (1987).

In terms of methodology, while both use statistical analysis and computer technology, the extent of such use and the types of tools employed differ somewhat across the two. As a branch of computer science dealing with language, computational linguistics focuses on doing formal modelling of natural language via computational algorithms and computer technology (Dipper, 2008; Wilks, 2010). In other words, the work of computational linguistics is based entirely on algorithms and technology, including the increased use of machine-learning technology. Machine-learning (which may be either supervised or unsupervised, an issue we will discuss in Section 2) refers to the practice of using algorithms to create a computational model based on sample data or training data for the purpose of making automatic inferences, predictions, or decisions (Shalev-Shwartz & Ben-David, 2014). Compared with conventional computational linguistics methods, machine-learning is more into achieving a higher level of automatic language processing, understanding, prediction, and production, and its algorithms may thus be more sophisticated. Compared with computational linguistics, corpus linguistics, while often also making use of algorithms and technologies, sometimes engages in substantial qualitative analysis with limited basic computations. However, it is important to note that the difference in methodology between computational and corpus linguistics has actually become much smaller in the past two decades because of the increasing use of computational models and tools, including those of machine-learning, by corpus linguists in their research and development of computerized language teaching and assessment programs, such as those used for automated essay scoring (e.g., ETS's *c-rater: www.ets.org/accelerate/ai-portfolio/c-rater*) and automated measuring of syntactic complexity (e.g., Lu, 2010). In short, overall, with the increased use of tools from computational linguistics by corpus linguists, there now seems to be a growing amount of overlap between the two disciplines.

1.3 Existing Work of Sentiment Analysis: Major Domains/Topics, Successes, Challenges/Questions, and Principles

This section contains three subsections. Section 1.3.1 introduces the domains where sentiment analysis has been conducted most extensively and the topics most frequently covered in each of the domains including the motivation behind them. Section 1.3.2 examines the successes of the existing work and the challenges/questions it has been facing. Section 1.3.3 discusses the key principles for conducting sentiment analysis. Some existing studies will be mentioned as examples to help illustrate the main points covered.

1.3.1 Major Domains and Topics

While sentiment analysis has been carried out in many different domains, business/finance, politics, healthcare/medicine, and entertainment (mainly movies) appear to be the four domains where it has been conducted and used most extensively (Feldman, 2013; Mäntylä et al., 2018; Rambocas & Pacheco, 2018; Zunic et al., 2020). A review of the published sentiment analysis studies in these four domains indicates that the topics or targets of sentiment analysis are domain specific with each domain having its own key topics. Table 1.1 lists the most frequently covered topics in each of the four domains plus the area of

Table 1.1 Main topics of sentiment analysis across domains

Domain	Common Topics	Major Data Sources	Amount of Existing Work
Business/ Finance	consumers/media/ businesses' opinions about the economy, financial markets, products, and services	online product/service reviews, surveys, business reports, and news	enormous
Politics	voters/public's opinions about candidates for elections, governments, legislations, policies, officials/politicians, and political parties	social media postings, news, polls, surveys, interviews, candidates' speeches and writings	enormous
Healthcare/ Medicine	patients' opinions, attitudes, and/or feelings about diseases and their diagnosis and treatments, medical services and providers, and medications	discussions on social media platforms, medical reports/other medical documents, reviews of healthcare services/medicines	large
Entertainment (movies)	reviewers' evaluations of movies including aspects of acting, cinematography, directing, music, script (plot/story), etc.	movie reviews	substantial
Academic writing/ applied linguistics	positivity/negativity in academic writing in general and across disciplines	journal articles, abstracts	limited

academic writing, a subfield of applied linguistics that has recently seen some sentiment analysis studies.[1] The latter is included our discussion because of its potential interest to the reader of this Element. Table 1.1 also presents the major data sources and the amount of existing work in each domain.

As displayed in Table 1.1, for business/finance, opinions about the economy, financial markets, products, and services constitute the key topics. The reason for the prominence of such topics in this domain is rather simple. Being entirely client dependent, companies must always know how customers feel about their products and/or services in order to maintain and increase their business. In fact, sentiment analysis results about products and services are not only important and useful for businesses but also for consumers in their purchase decision-making (Feldman, 2013; Mäntylä et al., 2018; Rambocas & Pacheco, 2018; Zhang et al., 2014). Similarly, finance firms and their clients need to understand how companies and investors feel about the economy/market and their future directions as well as about corporate financial performance so they can make informed investment decisions and be successful (Feldman, 2013; Ikoro et al., 2018; Loureiro, Bilro & Japutra, 2019; Rambocas & Pacheco, 2018). In fact, for those working in the stock market, an accurate understanding of sentiment about the market is crucial in making wise investment decisions (Garcia, 2013; Hajek, Olej & Myskova, 2014; Pagolu et al., 2016).

In the domain of politics, key topics include voter/public opinions about candidates for elections, governments, legislations, policies, officials/politicians, and political parties (Antonakaki et al., 2017; Jungherr et al., 2017; Murthy, 2015, Ramteke et al., 2016; Tumasjan et al., 2011; Unankard et al., 2014). The main reason that politics has generated a large number of sentiment analyses is that politics is public-opinion dependent and policy concerned, particularly during elections. Politicians, government agencies, and social/political organizations must constantly observe the sentiments of the public in order to win their support and/or to better serve the constituents they represent and govern. Furthermore, sentiment analysis before and during elections can provide valuable information for political parties and candidates to enhance their strategies for winning the election. The results of political sentiment analyses may also help predict election results, something that is of interest to not only the candidates and political parties involved but also the general public. The main sources of data for sentiment

---

[1] Sentiment analysis in academic writing here refers exclusively to those studies about the positivity/negativity in the published research articles expressed by their authors, not those studies that investigate the sentiments of the target subjects in an academic discipline for practical purposes, such as consumers' sentiments in business for the purposes of increasing sales or voters' sentiments in politics for the purpose of helping election candidates or predicting election outcomes.

analysis in politics include Twitter tweets and other social media postings as well as political candidates' interviews and speeches (Antonakaki et al., 2017; Jungherr et al., 2017; Liu & Lei, 2018).

Regarding the domain of healthcare/medicine, it is important to first note that healthcare is also a business, but a unique one because it has patients as its clients, medicines as its products, and treatments as its services provided by healthcare professionals (doctors and nurses). Hence, the main topics in this domain consist of patients' opinions and feelings about diseases and diagnoses/ treatments, healthcare services/providers, and medications (Oscar et al., 2017; Seabrook et al., 2018; Wang, Liu & Zhou, 2020). The importance of sentiment analysis in this domain lies in the following facts. First, healthcare providers and drug companies need to know how patients and the public view their products and services so they can make necessary improvements. Second, understanding the emotions and feelings of patients, especially mental health patients, is extremely important for successful treatment. In short, sentiment analysis in healthcare deals largely with patients' feelings and opinions about illnesses, medications, healthcare services, and treatments. It is also important to note that in terms of data used, sentiment analysis in this domain often includes not only patients' and healthcare professionals' postings on medical discussion plat-forms and social media but also medical reports and other documents that are not publicly available (Denecke & Deng, 2015; Weissman et al., 2019).

As for the entertainment domain, so far most of the sentiment analyses have focused on movies and the main topics, as can be expected, are reviewers' opinions about movies, especially the acting/actors, cinematography, directing, and music involved. It is important to note that most of these topics can be considered aspects of a movie that are often included in the sentiment analysis at the aspect level, as opposed to at the document or sentence level (a discussion of the three levels of sentiment analysis will be given in Section 2). Concerning the data source for sentiment analysis in this domain, movie reviews appear to have been essentially the only data used. Regarding the importance of sentiment analysis in this domain, clearly the results of such analysis are highly valuable for the entertainment industry and movie viewers. This is because often different reviews of a movie may diverge to various extents in their evaluations and it would be particularly helpful to learn the overall opinion of the reviews (i.e., systematic-ally generated opinion information via sentiment analysis). Such information can and has been used to predict movies' performance at the box office (Hur, Kang & Cho, 2016; Hu et al., 2018). This is important because most (i.e., 78 percent) of the movies produced each year are money losers (Davenport & Harris, 2009).

Academic writing, being an emerging area for sentiment analysis, has seen a few studies recently (Cao, Lei & Wen, 2020; Vinkers, Tijdink & Otte, 2015;

Weidmann, Otto & Kawerau, 2018). The areas of academic writing covered so far are limited to two: biomedical science (Cao et al., 2020; Vinkers et al., 2015) and political science (Weidmann et al., 2018) and the data used have been confined to journal articles and/or their abstracts. The methods employed have also been largely simple with a very small sentiment lexicon. However, these limited studies have all found a significant increase of positivity in academic writing and explored various interesting political and practical reasons for such an increase. Their results should have important practical implications for academic researchers.

1.3.2 Successes and Challenges

The tremendous efforts of researchers in the field of sentiment analysis have so far not only produced an enormous amount of work but also achieved some success in at least three areas. First, most of the existing studies have attained a sentiment identification accuracy ranging between 65 percent and 90 percent (Mukhtar, Khan & Chiragh, 2018; Rout et al., 2018; Zhang et al., 2014). This accuracy range, while clearly having room for enhancement, is fairly decent considering that the known reported accuracy or agreement of human sentiment judgment is 82 percent (Wilson, Wiebe & Hoffmann, 2005). Second, new fine-grained sentimental analysis tools and methods have been developed to help enhance the accuracy and effectiveness of sentiment identification and classification (e.g., Liang et al., 2015; Ren & Quan, 2012; Unankard et al., 2014). We will return to this point in Section 1.3.3. Third, some studies have demonstrated potentially useful practical applications of sentiment analysis, such as predicting election results, market performances, and product sales as well as identifying certain mental health conditions (e.g., Garcia, 2013; Giuntini et al., 2020, Sonnier, McAlister & Rutz, 2011; Tumasjan et al., 2011; Unankard et al. 2014).

For example, in the domain of business/finance, studies of how the sentiments in financial news (Garcia, 2013) and public opinions in tweets (Pagolu et al., 2016) forecast the movements of stock markets have demonstrated this predictive power. Similarly, both Liang et al.'s (2015) and Sonnier et al.'s (2011) studies on the relationship of customer reviews and product sales found that positive, negative, and neutral sentiments in customers' feedback all had a significant effect on sales. In the domain of politics, Tumasjan et al.'s (2011) sentiment analysis of Twitter messages concerning political parties and/or politicians during the 2009 German federal election revealed that the sentiments of voters' tweets about a political candidate were a good indicator of their political preferences and "the mere number of party mentions" accurately reflected the election result (p. 402). In another study, Unankard et al.

(2014) employed an approach that combined sentiment analysis of Twitter tweets with sub-event (i.e., an incident or crisis) identification to predict election results of the 2013 elections in Australia. They examined the effectiveness of the approach via a series of experiments and the results showed that their approach could "effectively predict the election results" (Unankard et al., 2014, p. 1).

In the domain of healthcare/medicine, Wang et al. (2020) developed a mental disorder identification model (MDI-Model) to help identify four different mental disorders, including depression and obsessive-compulsive disorder by analyzing the sequential emotion patterns of social media users over time in tweets written by disorder patients. Their results indicated high accuracy and efficiency of their MDI-Model in identifying the four types of mental disorders and the level of their severity. Seabrook et al. (2018), on the other hand, investigated how emotional states of "variability" and "instability" shown in Facebook and Twitter messages might reflect the severity of depression. Their results showed that instability in emotion was a significant indicator of more serious depressions while larger variability was a harbinger of lower depression severity.

While existing work of sentiment analysis has achieved some noticeable success as mentioned, there have also been some challenges and questions regarding its accuracy and predicting power as well as some other issues. In terms of sentiment identification accuracy, although the typical accuracy range is decent with a range of 65 percent to 90 percent as reported previously, much more work is needed to enhance this overall accuracy rate. Regarding the predictive power of sentiment analysis, despite some success as noted here, the results of a substantial number of studies (e.g., Gayo-Avello, 2012a, 2012b; Giuntini et al., 2020; Jungherr et al., 2017; Murphy, 2015; Rambocas and Pacheco, 2018; Weissman et al., 2019) have shown a lack or low level of such power, especially in the prediction of election results. Gayo-Avello (2012b), Jungherr et al. (2017), and Murphy (2015) all tried to use the results of sentiment analysis of election-related tweets to predict election outcomes, but they all failed. One reason for this failure, according to Murphy (2015, p. 816), was that the sentiments of political tweets were actually "more reactive rather than predictive." Even in the domain of business/finance, Rambocas and Pacheco's (2018) review of sentiment analysis studies in marketing published between 2008 and 2016 also revealed low validity and predictive power of such research. Similarly, in healthcare/medicine, Weissman et al.'s (2019) comparative study of six sentiment analysis methods applied to the texts of clinicians' encounter notes of patients with critical illness uncovered some serious issues with these methods, including their generally low predictive validity.

Underlying the accuracy and predictive power issues are some inherent language-usage-related difficulties for semantic analysis and classification. As is well known, language often involves anomalous usages that present challenges for natural language processing, such as double entendres, double negations, ironies, and sarcasms as shown in the following examples where the challenging words and structures in each example sentence are pointed out in the parentheses after it:

1. *The drill is boring* (both "drill" and "boring" have two different meanings).
2. *Rarely do I like that kind of movie* (inversion and adverb 'rarely" modifying the verb).
3. *I don't particularly dislike bananas* (double negation and restrictive adverb "particularly").
4. *Yeah, I really like him* (said sarcastically).
5. *I like this class, but probably won't recommend it to other students* (adversative conjunction "but" forming a qualified positive sentiment difficult to classify).

These language-usage-related difficulties are especially prevalent in the sentiment analysis of political discussions because, as Gayo-Avello (2012b, p. 93) points out, "[p]olitical discourse is plagued with humor, double entendres, and sarcasm." This fact often makes it difficult to ascertain individuals' political positions and voting intentions based on what they said or wrote.

A related important point to note is that some of the aforementioned language usage issues, such as negation (double negation), adverbial modifiers, and adversative conjunctions (e.g., "but" and "although") are part of the contextual information that sentiment analysis has to consider in its classification and calculation of the sentiment of a sentence or text. How to identify the different types of contextual information and factor them into sentiment analysis is part of the methodological/technological challenges or what Rambocas and Pacheco (2018) call "technical limitations" that sentiment analysis has been facing. The most noticeable methodology/technology-related challenges are inadequacies in the existing analysis tools, such as lexicons and training datasets (Zunic et al., 2020). These technical challenges will be discussed in Section 2.5 after an introduction of such tools in Sections 2.2–2.4 because some knowledge of these tools is needed to better understand the discussion.

Finally, there are some other challenges or questions regarding the interpretations and implications of the results of sentiment analysis. One concerns the fact that the same emotions or sentiments found in different texts might serve different purposes (Mohammad et al., 2015) and that negativity in sentiment might lead to an intended or unintended positive outcome while positivity might yield a negative one. For example, Liu and Lei's (2018) sentiment analysis of the campaign speeches of the 2016 US presidential candidates Hilary Clinton and Donald Trump found that Trump's speeches were significantly more negative than Clinton's, but his extreme negativity appeared to have appealed to his political base effectively helping him win the election. Another example can be found in Homburg, Ehm, and Artz's (2015) study on consumer sentiment by analyzing data from a company-sponsored online community forum and nine travel-related forums with active participation from not only consumers but also company representatives. Their results indicate that high-level active firm engagement actually had a negative effect on consumer sentiment. Such findings raise questions about how to interpret positive and negative sentiments and their actual practical implications.

1.3.3 Key Principles

The key principles for conducting sentiment analysis fall into two areas: data selection and methodology. Concerning data selection, existing studies and reviews (e.g., Giuntini et al., 2020; Hajek et al., 2014; Rambocas & Pacheco, 2018; Zunic et al., 2020) indicate that the data used should fit the research purpose and include different types when possible. Data selection typically involves a two-step decision process: (i) deciding what type(s) or source(s) of data would be most appropriate to use (e.g., whether to use economy-/finance-related Twitter tweets or annual/quarterly reports from companies or use both for a sentiment analysis of the financial market) and (ii) deciding what specific samples of the data to select (e.g., which specific tweets and/or reports to include). For example, in selecting data from social media postings for an election-related sentiment analysis, researchers have to consider not only which social media to include but also which specific postings to select based on a series of criteria, such as the mentioning of the word "election," the name(s) of the candidates, and/or the political parties involved. Similarly, while annual reports from companies have been found to be an important type of data because their sentiment "is an important forecasting determinant of financial performance" (Hajek et al., 2014, p. 721), a researcher still needs to decide which companies' reports from what time period to include. Hence using more than one source or type of data is common in sentiment analysis. For example, according to Zunic et al.'s (2020) systematic review of sentiment analyses in health and well-being, both social media postings (such as those on Twitter and Facebook) and discussions on web-based retailing platforms have been used in this line of research. Of course, what sources of data to use sometimes may be affected by the accessibility of the data involved and the level of ease with which the data of interest may be mined/obtained. This is because some data, such as medical reports and clinicians' notes, are generally not available to the public. In short, when it comes to data selecting for sentiment analysis, researchers should seek to include as large an amount of data from as many different appropriate sources as possible.

Similarly, for methodology-related principles, research has demonstrated that it is crucial to identify and extract the feature(s) that accurately reflect the sentiments of a text and it is also advisable to include a variety of features and use more than one analysis tools (e.g., more than one sentiment lexicon or algorithm) in one study. Doing so will significantly enhance the validity and accuracy of one's analysis. For example, in a study on the evaluation of consumer satisfaction, Ren and Quan (2012) examined not only emotion words but also the contextual linguistic information of such words in a sentence, such as adverbs. Furthermore, they developed "a fine-grained emotion recognition system" by using several different learning algorithms for measuring customer satisfaction (Ren & Quan, 2012, p. 322). As a result, they identified consumers' "blended" and "multiple" emotions and produced a more accurate assessment of consumer satisfaction. As another example, in the study of the campaign speeches of the 2016 US presidential election candidates mentioned previously, Liu and Lei (2018) employed two different lexicons in the computerized sentence-level sentiment analysis and also used structural topic modelling along with a *word2vec* examination to identify major themes and explore thematic associations. This multidimensional analysis enabled them to identify the two candidates' complex sentiments, discourse themes, and rhetoric strategies. Other studies that used multiple methods and techniques include Gonçalves, Benevenuto, and Cha (2013) and Rout et al. (2018), both of which employed supervised and unsupervised machine-learning approaches.

1.4 Summary

Sentiment analysis refers to the process of using algorithms and computer technologies to systematically detect, extract, and classify the subjective information and affective states expressed in a text. It is a rapidly growing research area with a range of applications across many different domains, especially in business, politics, healthcare/medicine, and entertainment. So far, sentiment analysis has attained some accuracy and shown some practical application potentials, but it still has substantial room for enhancement in both areas. Furthermore, it also still faces many other challenges, such as the difficulties involved with determining the sentiment of anomalous language usages and those usages whose meanings vary across contexts as well as many technical/

methodological limitations. There is no doubt, however, that sentiment analysis and its applications will continue to grow along with increasing efforts by researchers to address the existing challenges and enhance its success in the future.

2 Methods for Sentiment Analysis

2.1 Overview

There are essentially two major types of methods used for sentiment analysis: lexicon-based, now often called unsupervised machine-learning, and supervised machine-learning, along with the possibility of combining the two methods, i.e., a hybrid method (D'Andrea et al., 2015; Feldman, 2013; Mäntylä et al., 2018; Taboada et al., 2011; Zhang et al., 2014). Machine-learning sentiment analysis is a classification-based method that uses classification algorithms to identify the sentiment of a text. Such a method is used mainly for determining the polarity of a target document via automatic computing. This section provides a basic introduction to the two types of methods and an overview of the strengths and weaknesses of each.

Before we proceed, however, a brief discussion is in order concerning the levels of sentiment analysis that may be performed because they can vary across different sentiment analysis studies according to their purpose and/or focus. Overall, sentiment analysis may be carried out at three different levels: document level, sentence level, and aspect level (D'Andrea et al., 2015; Feldman, 2013; Unankard et al., 2014). As indicated by their names, document-level analysis assesses the overall sentiment of an entire document because it is generally believed that a document typically contains a main attitude or opinion about a given entity, issue, or topic being discussed. In comparison, sentence-level analysis evaluates the sentiment of a sentence. Therefore, sentence-level analysis renders more specific and fine-grained information than that provided by document-level analysis. Aspect-level analysis is conducted for "entities that have many aspects (attributes)," such as consumer products, since individuals often "have a different opinion about each of the aspects" of a product, such as the appearance, functionality, and price (Feldman, 2013, p. 85). As such, aspect analysis is especially useful for carrying out sentiment analysis of consumer products.

2.2 Unsupervised Machine-Learning/Lexicon-Based Methods

Before the concept of machine-learning was introduced, these methods were simply or exclusively called "lexicon-based" because of their use of a sentiment lexicon as the main tool for sentiment identification and classification. A sentiment lexicon is a word list that contains the target sentiment words coded as, among other things, positive, negative, or neutral, along with their respective level of strength or intensity. When such methods are used, machine-learning classification algorithms directly assess the target data with the assistance of a plugged-in sentiment lexicon to calculate a score for the sentiment of the document being evaluated based on the number and weighting of the sentiment words evaluated and tagged in the document. Figure 2.1 presents two examples of lexicon-based polarity assignments in the sentiment analysis of airline service reviews. The first shows a positive polarity value of 0.8659 assigned to the review being analyzed thanks to its use of the positive words *love/innovation/good.* The second indicates a negative polarity value of –0.1637 assigned to the review because of its use of the negative words *rude/bothered/unbelievable*. Given that *unbelievable* can actually be either positive or negative depending on the context, the assignment of negativity to *unbelievable* here indicates that the analysis took into consideration the negative context (i.e., the use of *rude/bothered* in the first sentence of the review).

It is important to note that in the machine-learning age today, lexicon-based methods are frequently labelled as "unsupervised machine-learning" because they do not include data training and the use of trained data where supervision is needed, a process that will be described later. However, their traditional name "lexicon-based" is still often used today. For clarity and consistency purposes, we adopt the term "unsupervised/lexicon-based" for our following discussion.

```
> ### POSITIVE
> mytext1 <- "@VirginAmerica I love the hipster innovation. You are a feel good brand."
> senti(mytext1)
[[1]]
   element_id word_count          sd ave_sentiment
1:          1         12 0.07101408     0.8658946
[[2]]
   element_id sentence_id        positive
1:          1           1 love,innovation
2:          1           2 good

> ### NEGATIVE
> mytext4 <- "@SouthwestAir customer service is rude and bothered by our calls. Has no idea what is going on
and sighed heavily on the phone. Unbelievable"
> senti(mytext4)
[[1]]
   element_id word_count         sd ave_sentiment
1:          1         24 0.4026705    -0.1637011
[[2]]
   element_id sentence_id      negative
1:          1           1 rude, bothered
2:          1           2
3:          1           3  unbelievable
```

Figure 2.1 Examples of polarity for airline service reviews

There are three approaches used to develop a sentiment lexicon: manual, corpus-based, and dictionary-based (D'Andrea et al., 2015; Taboada et al., 2011; Zhang et al., 2014). In the manual approach, the researcher(s) manually identify and code a list of sentiment words. As such, this approach is very time-consuming and hence rarely used alone today. Instead, it is often used together with the corpus-based or the dictionary-based approach, but its role is usually limited to double-checking the accuracy of the automated results from the latter approaches. In the corpus-based approach, a sentiment lexicon is developed by using a set of words whose sentiments or polarities are known as seeds to identify new sentiment words in a corpus based on the assumption that positive words may co-occur frequently with positive ones and negative words with negative ones. Specifically, the corpus-based approach uses statistical methods, such as pointwise mutual information (MI), to analyze and explore the semantic and syntactic relations between the seed words and their neighbouring words to extract a list of words closely associated with positive and negative polarities, hence resulting in a sentiment lexicon.

The dictionary-based approach, on the other hand, makes use of existing dictionary sources, such as WordNet, by first manually collecting a set of seed sentiment words and then searching a dictionary or dictionaries for the synonyms and antonyms of the seed words to expand the set into a desired lexicon. It is important to reiterate that the corpus-based and dictionary-based approaches are each often used together with the manual approach in the development of sentiment lexicons today (Tausczik & Pennebake, 2010; Zhang et al., 2014).

It is also worth noting that while some sentiment lexicons are meant for a specific domain (e.g., Hamilton et al.'s [2016] *SocialSent* lexicons for different social sciences), some others are intended for general or cross-domain use, such as Jockers' (2017b) *Syuzhet Lexicon*, Liu, Hu, and Cheng's (2005) *Bing Lexicon*, Tausczik and Pennebaker's (2010) *Linguistic Inquiry and Word Count (LIWC)*, and Taboada et al.'s (2011) *Semantic Orientation CALculator*. Yet, it is important to note that because language use varies greatly across domains and contexts, the use of cross-domain lexicons may often result in failing to identify semantic features that are unique and important for a given text or set of data being evaluated (Ramteke et al., 2016). Besides the aforementioned sentiment lexicons, there are some other well-known English sentiment lexicons, including *SentiWordNet*, *SentiWords*, *WordStat Sentiment Dictionary*, the *Affective Norms for English Words*, and the *Whissell Dictionary of Affect in Language*. In addition, there are now also many sentiment lexicons for other languages (cf. Chen & Skiena, 2014) and there have been new developments in emotion lexicons (e.g., Mohammad & Turney, 2010, 2013).

2.3 Supervised Machine-Learning Methods

The supervised machine-learning methods are techniques that classify the texts in the test dataset into one of the predefined sentiment categories based on the results of machine-learning from the training dataset. The process of supervised machine-learning is complex, but it may boil down to the following major steps for sentiment analysis. First, the texts of a target corpus are manually evaluated and coded for their sentiment polarities. Second, features that are considered distinctive of the texts or the sentiments of the texts, such as high-frequency words or phrases as well as other indices at syntactic or textual levels, are selected. It should be noted that features of a text at lexical, syntactic, and textual levels are diverse, and what features are selected for the machine to learn depends on the purpose of a given classification task, and more importantly, the expertise of the researchers. Third, the corpus of texts is divided into two sets – the training dataset and the test dataset. The machine is supervised to learn how the texts in the training dataset are classified as either positivity or negativity based on the selected features with machine-learning classification algorithms such as Decision Tree, Naïve Bayes, Random Forest, and Support Vector Machines (SVM). Last, the machine will classify texts in the test dataset, and the performance of the machine-learning models are evaluated with measures such as accuracy and precision (see Section 2.4 for a brief introduction to the measures). If the performance of the models is acceptable, the process of supervised machine-learning is completed and the models will be employed to classify other large-sized data. To recap, the supervised machine-learning process of sentiment analysis involves four steps: (1) manually evaluating the sentiment polarities of a corpus of data, (2) extracting the features based on the expertise of the researchers, (3) training an algorithm based on the examples (the training dataset), and (4) using the algorithm to compute the sentiment of the target document (the test dataset).

2.4 A Comparison of the Methods

Both unsupervised/lexicon-based and supervised machine-learning methods have their strengths and weaknesses. Regarding unsupervised/lexicon-based methods, because many existing lexicons are now readily available, it is generally a little easier for researchers to use such methods than supervised machine-learning methods. Furthermore, large cross-domain lexicons have also enabled such methods to provide a wider coverage than before. However, unsupervised/lexicon-based methods have two shortcomings. First, the number of items in a lexicon is generally limited, hindering its ability to extract senti-ment in texts from a variety of contexts; second, words in a sentiment lexicon are each usually assigned an invariable sentiment attribute and value, making them insensitive to how and where they are used (D'Andrea et al. 2015).

As for supervised machine-learning methods, their strength lies in their ability to develop new trained data or models for almost any given purpose and context (D'Andrea et al., 2015; Zhang et al., 2014). Yet supervised machine-learning methods also suffer from two weaknesses: one is the difficulty involved in integrating general semantic knowledge that has not been learned from the training data and the other is a lack of readily available labelled data, especially a lack of cross-domain data, that is, labelled data across business, medicine, and politics (D'Andrea et al., 2015; Zhang et al., 2014). The latter problem limits the applicability of supervised machine-learning across domains, which has led to some researchers' preference for unsupervised/lexicon-based methods (Taboada et al., 2011).

However, in general, so far there does not appear to be any consensus concerning whether unsupervised/lexicon-based or supervised machine-learning methods are more accurate and effective. While some studies (e.g., Zhang et al., 2014) have shown that supervised machine-learning methods perform better, a few others (e.g., Mukhtar et al., 2018) have found unsupervised lexicon-based methods to be more effective. A quick brief review of these studies should provide a better understanding of this issue. Zhang et al. (2014) did a two-part study: a review of existing research and an experimental study of their own comparing the performance of supervised learning and unsupervised/lexicon-based methods. In the former, the three supervised learning methods (i.e., three different classification algorithms) they reviewed all boasted an accuracy of 80 percent or above (86.40 percent, 82.52 percent, and 80.70 percent respectively), higher than the 74 percent yielded by the only unsupervised/lexicon-based approach study they reviewed that reported accuracy. The results of their own comparative study also showed that the two supervised machine-learning methods they used produced a higher accuracy (68.75 percent and 71 percent respectively) than the unsupervised/lexicon-based approach they included (64.25 percent).

In contrast, Mukhtar, Khan, and Chiragh's (2018) comparative study produced an opposite result. These researchers compared the performance of three supervised machine-learning methods with that of an unsupervised/lexicon-based approach in analyzing the sentiment in the Urdu blogging messages. They included four performance metrics in their analysis: accuracy, precision, recall, and F-score. Accuracy is the proportion of correctly annotated sentences to the total number of sentences in a text or corpus; precision is the proportion of correctly annotated sentences to the total number of **annotated** sentences; recall refers to the proportion of correctly annotated sentences to the total number of the sentences **that should have been correctly annotated**; F-score is a combined measure that tells how well a model performs by taking into account both recall and precision. The higher the value of each of an approach's four measures, the better the approach performs. Mukhtar et al.'s (2018) results showed that the unsupervised/lexicon-based method significantly outperformed the supervised machine-learning methods: while the former method achieved 89.03 percent accuracy, 0.86 precision, 0.90 recall, and 0.88 F-measure, the latter gained only 67.02 percent, 0.68, 0.67, and 0.67 in the four metrics respectively. The inconsistency in the results between this and the aforementioned two studies betrays the uncertainty about whether supervised machine-learning methods are indeed more effective.

These conflicting results about the accuracy issues related to the two types of methods seem to suggest that there is a danger that they both may either fail to identify or mislabel some sentiments in the target data. Given this fact, which method to use will depend on various factors, such as the domain and language being evaluated as well as the availability of a manually tagged dataset or a desired sentiment lexicon. This is because, as noted earlier, the availability of sentiment lexicons and trained data varies across domains and languages. For now, to help enhance the accuracy and effectiveness of one's study, a researcher can consider combining both unsupervised and supervised methods just as Gonçalves, Benevenuto, and Cha (2013) and Rout et al. (2018) have done. Of course, we can also expect that more enhanced methods and techniques will soon be developed because many researchers have been working on overcoming the existing challenges and have produced some very positive results as will be shown in the next section.

2.5 Challenges and Responses

One common problem facing both unsupervised/lexicon-based and supervised machine-learning methods is that while, on the one hand, many of the existing lexicons and training data are often limited to one domain, one context, and/or to one language (i.e., there is a lack of cross-domain tools), on the other hand, there is also the need for more specialized lexicons and training data that can catch sentiment features peculiar to a given domain or context. To address the former issue, researchers have been developing lexicons and training data that would work across domains and languages. For example, Chen and Skiena (2014) combined a variety of different linguistic resources to produce useful lexicons for 136 different languages. To help deal with the latter issue, researchers have been developing very specialized lexicons, such as Hamilton et al.'s (2016) *SocialSent* lexicons for various subfields of social sciences and

Yuan's (2017) petroleum lexicon. Studies have shown that specialized lexicons outperform general ones in domain/topic-specific analysis and that combining a general lexicon with a specialized lexicon can substantially improve success in sentiment analysis (e.g., Yekrangi & Abdolvand, 2020; Yuan 2017).

Another challenge in the development of lexicons and training data is the difficulty involved in the consideration and inclusion of some important factors in sentiment analysis, such as context, culture, and gender, which are common sources of variation in language use. As an example of cultural difference and the challenges it presents to sentiment analysis across contexts and languages, while "individualism" is a positive concept in English and other languages from individualistic cultures, it is viewed negatively in languages from collectivist cultures, such as Chinese and Japanese. Most of the existing lexicons and trained data are not very sensitive to variations caused by such factors. There have, however, been some suggestions on how to address this issue. For instance, to help better include contextual information, Rambocas and Pacheco (2018) suggest that machine-learning sentiment analysis integrate more manual analysis in sentiment classification by closely considering contextual information. To better cover cultural differences, Gopaldas (2014) proposed that large data companies, such as Google, employ more cultural anthropologists and clinical psychologists to help develop programs that can better build multimodal data and better identify linguistic variations. As an example for how this may work, the expertise of a cultural anthropologist should be able to assist in the development of a program that can correctly classify words whose sentiments vary across languages, such as "individualism" as mentioned previously. Finally, despite the effort to incorporate contextual information, no studies so far appear to have included phrases and Ngrams in their sentiment analysis. It should be of interest and importance to explore the inclusion of multiword units in sentiment analysis because research on evaluation in corpus linguistics has shown that phraseology plays an important role in evaluation (Hunston, 2011).

2.6 Summary

Unsupervised/lexicon-based and supervised machine-learning methods are two main approaches used in sentiment analysis. Each has its strengths and limitations. In terms of strength, while unsupervised/lexicon-based methods, with many existing lexicons readily available, are easier to use, especially for cross-domain analysis, supervised methods have the ability to develop any trained data for almost any given specific purpose and context. Regarding limitations, unsupervised/lexicon-based methods often suffer from the limited size of a lexicon and the fact that items in a lexicon are each usually assigned a fixed sentiment attribute or value insensitive to context. On the other hand, supervised methods have difficulty in integrating general semantic knowledge that has not been learned from the training data in their analysis and the problem of a lack of readily available labelled data, especially cross-domain data. Furthermore, both types of methods still have accuracy issues since they sometimes fail to identify or mislabel some sentiments in a text. Given this information, which method to use will depend on, among other factors, the purpose of a given sentiment analysis and the domain/language being analyzed. Of course, to enhance the accuracy and effectiveness of their studies, researchers can combine the two types of methods. Furthermore, as shown previously, encouragingly, many researchers have been developing and exploring new techniques and methodological innovations. More of such work can be expected in the future.

3 How to Do Sentiment Analysis with R

This section provides hands-on knowledge for conducting sentiment analysis using the R language. Concrete examples will be given to show, step-by-step, how to code R scripts for sentiment analysis. In this sense, this section aims to provide mainly the technical know-how of conducting sentiment analysis with R, not the interpretation and discussion of the results of the analysis and their implications. We will do the latter in Sections 4 and 5, two case studies of sentiment analysis.

This section is organized as follows. It begins with an example of supervised machine-learning sentiment analysis, then introduces two unsupervised/lexicon-based examples, one of sentiment analysis and one of emotion analysis. This section assumes a minimal knowledge of programming with R (i.e., knowing the major R data structures of vectors and data frames and basic skills in writing and running scripts in R). For such basic knowledge, readers who are new to R may refer to the two following free courses on Coursera: Getting Started with R (www.coursera.org/projects/getting-started-with-r) and Data Science: Foundations using R (www.coursera.org/specializations/data-science-foundations-r).

3.1 Supervised Machine-Learning Sentiment Analysis with R

In Section 2, we discussed two main methods for sentiment analysis: unsupervised/lexicon-based and supervised machine-learning. In this section, a step-by-step example of supervised learning sentiment analysis is provided.

3.1.1 Process of Supervised Machine-Learning Sentiment Analysis

The process of supervised machine-learning sentiment analysis includes four stages: (1) data preparation, (2) data training, (3) prediction, and (4) classification of the main target data (see Table 3.1). In the data preparation stage, we first collect the data that are to be used for sentiment analysis, and then manually tag the sentiments of each text of the data as "positive" or "negative." For example, for a large dataset of a million tweets on a certain topic, we may randomly extract a smaller part of the dataset (e.g., 10,000 tweets) and manually tag the sentiments of the 10,000 tweets as "positive" or "negative.. Then, we train the model and ask the machine (i.e., a chosen algorithm) to automatically classify the 10,000 tweets. If the accuracy of the machine-learning model is acceptable (e.g., 90 percent), then we use the model to automatically tag the remaining 90,000 tweets.

At the training stage, we first extract the features of the data, particularly the linguistic features at the word level and the phrasal level (i.e., Ngrams, such as bigrams or trigrams) including their respective frequencies as well as syntactic patterns. Then, we separate the dataset (take the 10,000 manually tagged tweets as the example again) into the training set and the testing set. Most of the time, the training set may take up 70–80 percent of the data, while the testing set is the remaining 20–30 percent (e.g., 7,500 tweets for the training set and 2,500 for the testing set). Using a machine-learning algorithm such as Naïve Bayes or Support Vector Machine, we train the training dataset (the 7,500 tweets) and obtain a machine-learning model after training the data. At the prediction stage, based on the machine-learning model we have obtained from the training stage, we let the machine automatically classify the testing dataset (the 2,500 tweets). The results of the automatic classification will be compared with those of the manual tagging and the accuracy of the automatic classification is calculated. If the accuracy is acceptable, we move to the final stage by using the model to classify the larger part of the dataset (the remaining 90,000 tweets). Otherwise, the model will be retested and improved with other experiments and based on other methods, such as trials of other features or other algorithms.

Table 3.1 Process of machine-learning

1. Data preparation	1.1 Data collection
	1.2 Manual tagging
2. Training	2.1 Feature extraction
	2.2 Modelling the training dataset
3. Prediction	3 Classifying the training dataset
4. Classification of the main data	4 If model accuracy is acceptable, classify the larger part of the data; else, go to step 2.1

3.1.2 Doing Supervised Machine-Learning Sentiment Analysis with R

In this section, we conduct an experiment of supervised machine-learning sentiment analysis with R. The data we use is the open dataset of Twitter US Airline Sentiment (downloaded from www.kaggle.com/crowdflower/twitter-airline-sentiment). It contains a total of 14,640 tweets of travellers' attitudes toward the services of six American airlines: American, Delta, Southwest, United, US Airways, and Virgin America. Each tweet in the dataset was manually tagged with its sentiment polarity, such as "positive," "negative," or "neutral," making the dataset ideal for an experiment of supervised machine-learning sentiment analysis. The dataset is stored in a .csv file named "airline_tweets.csv."

To begin with our experiment, we first load all the packages we need (See Code 3.1).

Code 3.1

```
library("dplyr")
library("readr")
library("tm")
library("wordcloud")
library("e1071")
library("caret")
```

Then, we read the file of the experiment dataset in, and the data is now stored in a data frame named "data" (Code 3.2). A data frame is a data structure in R that is spreadsheet-like, most often with columns as the variables and with rows as the cases. Note that we provide both the codes and results in the code boxes (see Code 3.3), with the codes at the beginning followed by the results (the same practice in all the following code boxes hereafter; however, due to space limits, we omitted some parts of the results in some code boxes when the omission did not appear to affect understanding of the results). That is, the lines beginning "> " are the codes and the other lines are the results of the codes. When the readers type in the codes in their RStudio, they do not need to type "> ."

Code 3.2

```
> path <- "D:/"
> data <- read_csv(paste0(path, "airline_tweets.csv"))
```

We can use the `glimpse()` function to take a quick look at the structure of the data frame (Code 3.3). We can see from the results that the dataset contains 15 columns and a total of 14,640 rows. For example, the `airline_senti-ment` row includes the manually tagged sentiments of each tweet and the `text` row is composed of travellers' tweet texts.

Code 3.3

```
> glimpse(data)
Rows: 14,640
Columns: 15
$ tweet_id <dbl> 5.70306e+17, 5.70301e+17, 5.70301e+17, 5...
$ airline_sentiment <chr> "neutral", "positive", "neutral",
"negat...
$ airline_sentiment_confidence <dbl> 1.0000, 0.3486, 0.6837,
1.0000, 1.0000, ...
$ negativereason <chr> NA, NA, NA, "Bad Flight", "Can't Tell",
...
$ negativereason_confidence <dbl> NA, 0.0000, NA, 0.7033,
1.0000, 0.6842, ...
...
```

Since we are aiming to predict the sentiments of the tweet texts in the experiment, the rows that we need for the experiment are the `airline_sen-timent` row and the `text` one. Also, we only use two sentiments in the experiment – "positive" and "negative" – and the data that include sentiment "neutral" are filtered out (see Code 3.4). Note that the "+ " means the previous line of function is not complete and the line starting with "+ " continues with the previous one. Hence, when the readers type the code, "+ " is, similar to ">, " not needed.

Code 3.4

```
> #select the columns: tweets and sentiments
> df <- data %>%
+ select(airline_sentiment = airline_sentiment,
+ text = text) %>%
+ filter(airline_sentiment != "neutral")
```

If we want to know how many positive and negative tweets as well as their proportions are used in the training data of this experiment, we may use the table() and the prop.table() functions to accomplish it (Code 3.5). From the results, we learn that there are 9,178 negative tweets (79.53 percent) and 2,363 positive ones (20.47 percent).

Code 3.5

```
> table(df$airline_sentiment)

negative positive
  9178 2363

> prop.table(table(df$airline_sentiment))

negative positive
0.7952517 0.2047483
```

The next step is to extract the features of the tweets for the follow-up sentiment training and classification. For this experiment, we argue that the high-frequency words occurring in the tweets may play important roles in the tweets. That is, high-frequency words may serve as distinctive sentiment features in the tweets. To extract the high-frequency words as features, we first convert the texts of the tweets into a corpus, with the aid of the Corpus() function in the tm package. Then, we check the first three tweets in the corpus with the inspect() function[2] (Code 3.6).

Code 3.6

```
> #convert the tweets texts into a corpus

> corpus <- Corpus(VectorSource(df$text))

> inspect(corpus[1:3])
≪SimpleCorpus≫
Metadata: corpus specific: 1, document level (indexed): 0
Content: documents: 3

[1] @VirginAmerica plus you've added commercials to the
experience ... tacky.
[2] @VirginAmerica it's really aggressive to blast obnoxious
"entertainment" in your guests' faces &amp; they have little
recourse
[3] @VirginAmerica and it's a really big bad thing about it
```

---

[2] Some of the following codes are adapted from Katti (2016). We would like to express our sincere thanks to Rohit Katti.

The next task is to clean the data since the words serving as the features should not include such things as stop words (e.g., *the* and *her*) and numbers, as well as punctuations and spaces (Code 3.7).

Code 3.7

```
> # data cleaning
> corpus_clean <- corpus %>%
+ tm_map(content_transformer(tolower)) %>%
+ tm_map(removePunctuation) %>%
+ tm_map(removeNumbers) %>%
+ tm_map(removeWords, stopwords(kind="en")) %>%
+ tm_map(stripWhitespace)
```

Then, we model the Document Term Matrix (DTM). The DTM is a matrix or a spreadsheet-like data structure which represents a bag of words. The rows of the matrix are the IDs of documents in the data (in this case, the tweet ids), and the columns are the terms (in the present case, the words minus numbers and stop words). The elements or the cells in the spreadsheet are the frequencies of the words. We model the DTM with the `DocumentTermMatrix()` function in the `tm` package. Again, we use the `inspect()` function to view the matrix (rows 1:8, columns 10:16, i.e., words #10 to #16 in tweets #1 to #8) (Code 3.8). It is obvious that many words do not occur in most documents or tweets. Hence, the DTM is most often a sparse matrix.

Code 3.8

```
> #to develop the dtm model and choose the features of high
frequency words

> dtm <- DocumentTermMatrix(corpus_clean)

> inspect(dtm[1:8, 10:16])
≪DocumentTermMatrix (documents: 8, terms: 7)≫
Non-/sparse entries: 9/47
Sparsity : 84%
Maximal term length: 13
Weighting : term frequency (tf)
Sample :
   Terms
Docs blast entertainment faces guests little obnoxious
really
```

```
1 0 0 0 0 0 0 0
2 1 1 1 1 1 1 1
3 0 0 0 0 0 0 1
4 0 0 0 0 0 0 1
5 0 0 0 0 0 0 0
6 0 0 0 0 0 0 0
7 0 0 0 0 0 0 0
8 0 0 0 0 0 0 0
```

If we want to know the most frequent words, we first calculate the total frequency of each word, and convert the word-frequency matrix into a data frame with a decreasing order of word frequency. The results of Code 3.9 show the 12 most frequent words in the tweets texts with their frequencies.

Code 3.9

```
> ### most highly frequent words
> dtm_matrix <- as.matrix(dtm)

> dtm_frequency_sort <- sort(colSums(dtm_matrix),
+ decreasing = TRUE)
> df_frequency <- data.frame(word =
names(dtm_frequency_ sort),
+ freq = dtm_frequency_sort)

> head(df_frequency, 12)
  word freq
united united 3395
flight flight 3314
usairways usairways 2642
americanair americanair 2443
southwestair southwestair 1779
jetblue jetblue 1612
get get 1105
cancelled cancelled 962
now now 916
thanks thanks 916
service service 901
just just 805
```

We can also make a word cloud based on the data frame of word frequency, with the wordcloud() function in the wordcloud package. The word cloud resulting from Code 3.10 is illustrated in Figure 3.1.

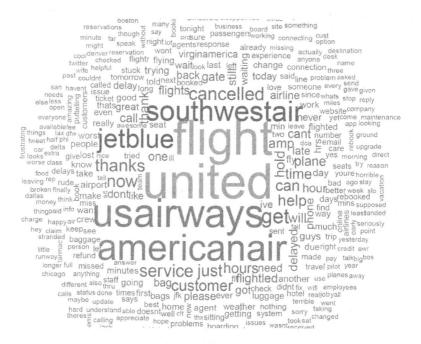

Figure 3.1 Word cloud

Code 3.10

```
# word cloud
wordcloud(words = df_frequency$word,
  freq = df_frequency$freq,
  min.freq = 50,
  random.order = FALSE,
  colors = brewer.pal(6, "Dark2"))
```

Now, we split the data into a training set and a testing set. In this case, we hope that 75 percent of the data are assigned to the training dataset. Since we have a total of 11,541 tweet texts, 75 percent (i.e., 8,656) of them are assigned to the training dataset. The remaining tweet texts are assigned to the testing set (Code 3.11).

Code 3.11

```
> # split the data
> set.seed(2021)
```

```
> train_sample_id <- sample(1:11541, 8656)

> df_train <- df[train_sample_id,]
> df_test <- df[-train_sample_id,]
> dtm_train <- dtm[train_sample_id,]
> dtm_test <- dtm[-train_sample_id,]

> corpus_clean_train <- corpus_clean[train_sample_id]
> corpus_clean_test <- corpus_clean[-train_sample_id]

> # Use high frequent words to build the DTM

> dtm_train <- DocumentTermMatrix(corpus_clean_train,
+ control=list(dictionary = high_freq))

> dtm_test <- DocumentTermMatrix(corpus_clean_test,
+ control=list(dictionary = high_freq))
```

In this experiment, we believe that the factor of "occurrence or no occurrence" of the feature words is more important than that of their frequencies for the classification or prediction of the sentiments in a tweet text. Hence, we define a function to convert their frequencies to "Yes" (if the frequency is larger than 0) or "No" (if the frequency is 0). Then, we apply the function to convert the frequencies to "Yes" or "No" (Code 3.12).

Code 3.12

```
> # Develop a function to convert word frequencies to Yes or No

> convert_count <- function(x) {
+ y <- ifelse(x > 0, 1,0)
+ y <- factor(y, levels=c(0,1), labels=c("No", "Yes"))
+ y
+ }

> # convert word frequencies to Yes or No

> dtm_train_final <- apply(dtm_train, 2, convert_count)
> dtm_test_final <- apply(dtm_test, 2, convert_count)

> train_features <- as.data.frame(dtm_train_final)
> train_sentiments <- as.factor(df_train$airline_sentiment)
> test_features_sentiments <- as.data.frame(dtm_test_
final) %>%
+ mutate(airline_sentiment = as.factor(df_test
$airline_sentiment))
```

Now, it is time to train the classifier model. In this experiment, we use the Naïve Bayes algorithm to train the model based on the training dataset with the `naiveBayes()` function in the `e1071` package (Code 3.13). The Naïve Bayes algorithm is a simple but robust technique which is widely used to develop classification models or classifiers based on selected features.

Code 3.13

```
> # Train the classifier model
> model <- naiveBayes(train_features, train_sentiments,
laplace = 1)
```

Then, we use the trained model to predict the sentiments of the data in the testing dataset with the `predict()` function (Code 3.14).

Code 3.14

```
> #Testing the Predictions
> prediction <- predict(model, newdata =
test_features_sentiments)
```

Afterwards, we use the `confusionMatrix()` function in the `caret` package to calculate the confusion matrix and the prediction accuracy (Code 3.15). The results indicate that the overall accuracy is 90.68 percent. Of all the tweets tagged with "negative" in the testing dataset, 2,142 were automatically correctly tagged while 164 were tagged incorrectly. For the "positive" tweets in the testing dataset, 474 were tagged correctly and 105 were tagged incorrectly. The results mean that the model is more than acceptable. Now we are ready to use the model to classify or compute the sentiment of the larger or main dataset.

Code 3.15

```
> #Confusion Matrix
> confusion_matrix <- confusionMatrix(prediction, test_
features_sentiments$airline_sentiment)

> confusion_matrix$overall['Accuracy']
  Accuracy
0.9067591
```

Table 3.2 Results of the supervised machine-learning sentiment analysis

Corpus size	14,640 tweets
Manually annotated negative tweets	9,178
Manually annotated positive tweets	2,363
Manually annotated neutral tweets (excluded in the analysis)	3,099
Features selected	High-frequency words
Training set (75% of the manually positive or negative tweets, 11,541 in total)	8,656
Testing set (25% of the manually positive or negative tweets, 11,541 in total)	2,885
"Positive" tweets: machine annotated positive	474/579
"Positive" tweets: machine annotated negative	105/579
"Negative" tweets: machine annotated negative	2,142/2,306
"Negative" tweets: machine annotated positive	164/2,306
Accuracy	2,616/2,885 = 0.9067591

As noted, the overall accuracy of the trained model is 90.68 percent, which is considered acceptable. Of course, the researchers may also experiment on other features such as multi-word chunks or Ngrams with other machine-learning algorithms, such as Logistic Regression or Support Vector Machine to improve the accuracy. To help the reader better understand the process of how the output (i.e., the accuracy) in Code 3.15 was generated, we have summarized the results of the machine-learning sentiment analysis of the Twitter US Airline corpus in Table 3.2.

3.2 Unsupervised/Lexicon-Based Sentiment Analysis

In this section, we present the methods for doing unsupervised/lexicon-based sentiment analysis with a concrete example.

3.2.1 Rationale of Unsupervised/Lexicon-Based Sentiment Analysis

As we discussed in the previous section, the unsupervised/lexicon-based approach to sentiment analysis uses a sentiment lexicon to help determine the sentiment of a target text. A lexicon can be specialized focusing on one domain or cross-domain with a large number of sentiment words that are domain neutral (D'Andrea et al., 2015), that is, they can be applied across domains. Hence, researchers often prefer to use a lexicon-based approach with a large cross-domain lexicon for conducting sentiment analysis of nonspecialized language data (Taboada et al., 2011).

As already mentioned in the last section, there are quite a few ready-to-use large cross-domain lexicons. For example, there are many built-in lexicons in popular sentiment analysis R packages, such as `syuzhet` (Jockers, 2017a) and `sentimentr` (Rinker, 2018). These lexicons vary in the number of sentiment words included as well as sentiment values or valences used. See Table 3.3 for a summary of the lexicons.

The packages `syuzhet` (Jockers, 2017a) and `sentimentr` (Rinker, 2018) are largely similar. That is, they provide robust functions for unsupervised/lexicon-based sentiment analysis and have been used in research in various domains for different purposes, such as analyzing campaign speech discourse in politics (e.g., Liu & Lei, 2018), customers' and companies' bloggings and tweets in business (e.g., Ikoro et al., 2018), and doctors' clinical notes and patients' messages at online discussion platforms in medicine (e.g., Weissman et al., 2019). However, `sentimentr` (Rinker, 2018) is different from `syuzhet` (Jockers, 2017a) in that `sentimentr` (Rinker, 2018) considers valence shifters. For example, if a sentence has a negator (e.g., *not*), an intensifier (e.g., *highly*), a downtoner (e.g., *slightly*), or an adversative conjunction (e.g., *however*), the valence shifter in `sentimentr`

Table 3.3 Sentiment lexicons provided by `syuzhet` (Jockers, 2017a) and `sentimentr` (Rinker, 2018)

Lexicon title	Number of sentiment words	Sentiment values/ valences
Syuzhet (Jockers, 2017b)	10,748	−1 to +1
AFINN (Nielsen, 2011)	2,477	−5 to +5
Bing (Hu & Liu, 2004; B. Liu et al., 2005)	6,789	−1 to +1
NRC (Mohammad & Turney, 2010, 2013)	13,901	"positive" or "negative"
SenticNet (Cambria et al., 2016)	23,626	−1 to +1

(Rinker, 2018) would work and incorporate weighting on or adjusting the sentiment value of the sentence. Based on such a mechanism of valence shifting, the accuracy of sentiments measured with `sentimentr` (Rinker, 2018) may be higher. Hence, `sentimentr` (Rinker, 2018) is used in this Element to demonstrate how to do lexicon-based sentiment analysis with R.

3.2.2 Doing Unsupervised/Lexicon-Based Sentiment Analysis with R

The data that we use in this demonstration experiment are the same as those used in Section 3.1.2, that is, the open dataset of Twitter US Airline Sentiment. Let us start with installing and loading of the R packages that we need for this experiment (Code 3.16).

Code 3.16

```
library("dplyr")
library("readr")
library("sentimentr")
```

Then, similar to what was done in the previous section, we first read in the dataset of Twitter US Airline Sentiment from the .csv file, select the columns of the tweet texts, and filter out the rows or cases that were manually tagged as "neutral" (Code 3.17). The read-in dataset is now stored in a data frame named `df`.

Code 3.17

```
> path <- "D:/"
> data <- read_csv(paste0(path, "airline_tweets.csv"))
> #select the columns: tweets and sentiments
> df <- data %>%
  select(airline_sentiment = airline_sentiment,
  text = text) %>%
  filter(airline_sentiment != "neutral")
```

We now experiment the unsupervised/machine-learning approach to computing and determining the sentiment of a sentence. For illustration purposes, we use the third tweet text in the database as an example. We first use `df$text` [3] to extract the text and store the text in the variable `mytext`. The result shows that the third tweet text is "@VirginAmerica and it's a really big bad thing about it" (Code 3.18).

Different from the approach of supervised machine-learning sentiment analysis we introduced in the previous section, determining the sentiment of a sentence with an unsupervised/lexicon-based method is much more straightforward. For the R package `sentimentr` (Rinker, 2018), we directly use the `sentiment_by()` function to tag the text and compute the sentiment. The result shows that the text contains ten words (`word_count: 10`) and the sentiment value is –0.284605 (`ave_sentiment: -0.284605`), that is, a negative value, which indicates that the sentiment of the tweet sentence/text is automatically measured as negative. The tagging/computing result confirms our intuition on the sentiment of the sentence.

It should be noted that the `sentiment_by()` function uses, by default, a combined lexicon consisting of the `syuzhet` lexicon (Jockers, 2017b) and Rinker's (2018) lexicon. If we want to use other lexicons, we may set the parameter `polarity_dt` in the function. As the script in Code 3.18 shows, for example, we set the parameter to `lexicon::hash_sentiment_senticnet` in order to use the `SenticNet` lexicon (Cambria et al., 2016). The sentiment value of the tweet text based on the `SenticNet` lexicon is also negative, though the value is slightly different, probably due to the difference in the sentiment values assigned to the sentiment words between the two lexicons.

Code 3.18

```
# tag a sentence
> mytext <- df$text[3]
> mytext
[1] "@VirginAmerica and it's a really big bad thing about it"
> sentiment_by(mytext)
   element_id word_count sd ave_sentiment
1: 1 10 NA -0.284605
> sentiment_by(mytext, polarity_dt =
lexicon::hash_sentiment_senticnet)
   element_id word_count sd ave_sentiment
1: 1 10 NA -0.1479946
```

One function of the `sentimentr` package (Rinker, 2018) that may be of pedagogical interest is its visualisation of the results of sentiment analysis. For example, in Code 3.19, we first extract the fourth and sixth tweet texts from the dataset (`df$text[c(4, 6)]`). Then, we check their manually tagged sentiments (`df$airline_sentiment[c(4,6)]`), which results with the fourth text as "negative" and the sixth as "positive." Next, we check what the two tweet texts are with `mytext2`. Last, we perform the sentiment analysis of the two texts with the function `sentiment_by()` and visualize the results with the function

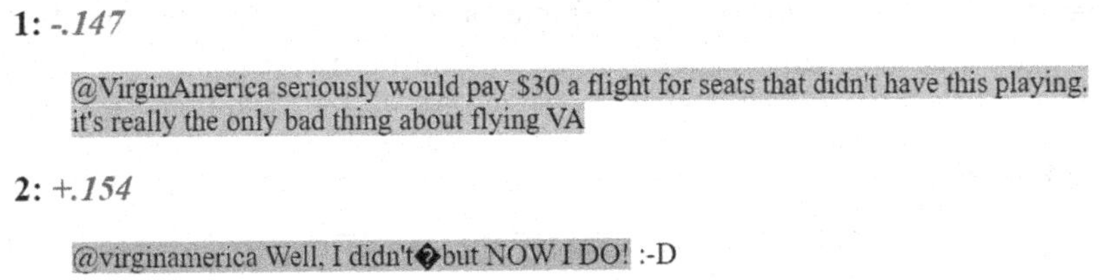

1: -.*147*

@VirginAmerica seriously would pay $30 a flight for seats that didn't have this playing. it's really the only bad thing about flying VA

2: +.*154*

@virginamerica Well, I didn't◆but NOW I DO! :-D

Figure 3.2 Visualization of sentiment analysis

highlight(). The visualization will automatically pop up in the default browser of our system (Figure 3.2). As Figure 3.2 shows, the fourth tweet text (Sentence 1 in the figure) is in red font since its sentiment value is negative (–0.147), and the sixth tweet text (Sentence 2 in the figure) is in green font because its sentiment value is positive (0.154).

Code 3.19

```
> # A Fun: to highlight the positive and negative sentences
> mytext2 <- df$text[c(4, 6)]

> df$airline_sentiment[c(4,6)]
[1] "negative" "positive"

> mytext2
[1] "@VirginAmerica seriously would pay $30 a flight for seats
that didn't have this playing.\nit's really the only bad thing
about flying VA"
[2] "@virginamerica Well, I didn't ... but NOW I DO! :-D"

> sentences <- get_sentences(mytext2)
> sentiment_by(sentences) %>%
+ highlight()
Saved in
C:\Users\Leo\AppData\Local\Temp\RtmpgHyVv1/polarity.html
Opening
C:\Users\Leo\AppData\Local\Temp\RtmpgHyVv1/polarity.html
...
```

In the next snippet of code, we demonstrate how to code and compute the sentiments of a series of sentences. We may use the head() function to check out the first six items of a series of data (in this case, the first six tweet texts of the dataset). As the result of Code 3.20 shows, the head() function returns a data frame or a table of six rows and two columns (the manually tagged sentiments and the tweet texts).

Code 3.20

```
> # tag the first six tweets
> head(df)
# A tibble: 6 x 2
  airline_sentiment text
  <chr> <chr>
1 positive "@VirginAmerica plus you've added commercials to
the experien~
2 negative "@VirginAmerica it's really aggressive to blast
obnoxious \"e~
...
```

Since the head() function does not show the complete texts of the tweets, we can use head(df$text) to view the complete texts (Code 3.21). Similarly, we can use head(df$airline_sentiment) to see the manually coded sentiments of the six tweet texts.

Code 3.21

```
> head(df$text)
[1] "@VirginAmerica plus you've added commercials to the
experience ... tacky."
[2] "@VirginAmerica it's really aggressive to blast
obnoxious \"entertainment\" in your guests' faces &amp; they
have
little recourse"
...

> head(df$airline_sentiment)
[1] "positive" "negative" "negative" "negative" "positive"
"positive"
```

Now, let us conduct sentiment analysis on the six tweet texts, again with the sentiment_by() function (Code 3.22). The results of the sentiment analysis are now stored in a data frame named "df_head." Then, we add the manually tagged sentiments of the tweet texts to the data frame in order to compare the manually coded sentiments with the automatically classified sentiments based on the plugged-in lexicon (`mutate(original_senti-ment = head(df$airline_sentiment))`).

Code 3.22

```
df_head <- sentiment_by(head(df$text))
> # add the orignal sentiments
> df_head_sentiments <- df_head %>%
+ mutate(original_sentiment
= head(df$airline_sentiment)) %>%
+ select(-sd)
> df_head_sentiments
   element_id word_count ave_sentiment original_sentiment
1: 1 9-0.1364216 positive
2: 2 17-0.5893616 negative
3: 3 10-0.2846050 negative
4: 4 22-0.1466282 negative
5: 5 15 0.2711088 positive
6: 6 9 0.1543434 positive
```

The results indicate that five of the manually and automatically tagged sentiments (from the second to the sixth) are the same, while the results of the first text are different, with its manually tagged sentiment being "positive" and its automatically tagged sentiment being "negative." Let us look at the first tweet text again (Code 3.23). We hypothesize that the word "tacky" may play a decisive role if the sentence is tagged as "negative." Thus, we check the sentiment of the word "tacky." The result shows that the sentiment value of the word is –0.25, which is "negative." To further test our hypothesis, we examine which word/s is/are responsible for the "negative" sentiment of the tweet text with the `extract_sentiment_terms()` function. The result confirms our hypothesis: it is indeed the word "tacky" that is responsible for the negativity of the text.

A comparison of the manually tagged sentiments that are originally provided in the dataset and the automatically tagged ones is of great importance. This is because, the originally provided sentiments were manually tagged and hence may be subjective and debatable. For example, the sentiment of the first tweet text was originally manually tagged as "positive," but it may be classified as negative by an automatic tagging tool as shown in the previous result. In other words, manually tagged sentiments of sentences or texts may sometimes be different from the machine tagged ones, which in turn shows the complexity involved in sentiment analysis.

Code 3.23

```
> df$text [1]
[1] "@VirginAmerica plus you've added commercials to the
experience ... tacky."
> sentiment_by("tacky")
  element_id word_count sd ave_sentiment
1: 1 1 NA -0.25

> extract_sentiment_terms(df$text[1])
  element_id sentence_id negative
1: 1 1
2: 1 2 tacky
```

Now, let us classify and compute the sentiments of all tweet texts in the entire dataset with sentiment_by() (Code 3.24). Then, we add the original tweet texts with the mutate() function and take a quick look at it with the glimpse() function. If we want to save the results, we can use the write_csv() function to write the results out in a .csv file.

Code 3.24

```
> df_all <- sentiment_by(df$text)

> # add the original tweet texts
> df_all_sentiments <- df_all %>%
+ mutate(tweet_text = df$text) %>%
+ select(-sd)
> glimpse(df_all_sentiments)
Rows: 11,541
Columns: 4
$ element_id <int> 1, 2, 3, ...
$ word_count <int> 9, 17, 10, ...
$ ave_sentiment <dbl> -0.136421582, -0.589361569,
-0.284604989, ...
$ tweet_text <chr> "@VirginAmerica plus you've added
commercials to the ex ...

write_csv(df_all_sentiments, paste0(path,
"airline_sentiments_lexicon_results.csv"))
```

Table 3.4 Results of the unsupervised/lexicon-based sentiment analysis

Corpus size	14,640 tweets
Manually annotated negative tweets	9,178
Manually annotated positive tweets	2,363
Manually annotated neutral tweets (excluded in the lexicon-based analysis)	3,099
Lexicon used	*senticnet*
Number of sentiment words in *senticnet*	23,626
Sentiment values/valences range	-1 to $+1$
Sentiment values/valences $>=0.10$	4,092
Sentiment values/valences $>=0.25$	1,926
Sentiment values/valences $<=-0.10$	3,340
Sentiment values/valences $<=-0.25$	1,275

To help the reader better understand how the output in Code 3.24 was generated, we have summarized the results of the unsupervised/lexicon-based sentiment analysis of the Twitter Airline corpus in Table 3.4.

If we want to view the tweet text with the highest positive value, we can extract it with the `filter()` and the `max()` functions (Code 3.25). As the results indicate, the text with the highest positive aggregate value is "@united … But friendly efficient air attendants in coach #UA992 http://t.co/ 49pV3KcHNR," with a sentiment value at 1.14.

Code 3.25

```
> df_all_sentiments %>%
+ filter(ave_sentiment == max(ave_sentiment))
  element_id word_count ave_sentiment
1: 1029 14 1.142675
  tweet_text
1: @united ... But friendly efficient air attendants in coach
#UA992 http://t.co/49pV3KcHNR
```

If we want to see more tweet texts with high positive values, we can first sort the data frame by the sentiments with a descending order (`arrange(desc(ave_sentiment))`), and then extract the first six rows with the `head()` function (Code 3.26).

Code 3.26

```
> df_all_sentiments %>%
+ arrange(desc(ave_sentiment)) %>%
+ head()
   element_id word_count ave_sentiment
1: 1029 14 1.142675
2: 1173 9 1.125000
3: 2891 6 1.122683
4: 2998 23 1.111382
5: 3119 3 1.068098
6: 976 2 1.060660
...
   original_sentiment
1: negative
2: positive
3: positive
4: positive
5: positive
6: negative
```

The other way around is to check the tweet texts with the most negative values. To do so, we can first sort the data frame by the sentiments with a descending order, and then extract the last six rows with the `tail()` function (Code 3.27).

Code 3.27

```
> df_all_sentiments %>%
+ arrange(desc(ave_sentiment)) %>%
+ tail()
   element_id word_count ave_sentiment
1: 705 22 -1.140453
2: 6117 23 -1.165074
3: 10289 20 -1.182321
4: 10932 13 -1.258125
5: 10325 20 -1.271764
6: 8486 13 -1.323252
tweet_text
...
   original_sentiment
1: negative
2: negative
```

```
3: negative
4: negative
5: positive
6: negative
```

3.3 Unsupervised/Lexicon-Based Emotion Analysis

As discussed in the last section, emotion analysis, an important component of sentiment analysis, provides detailed indices of the feelings expressed in a text about a given thing or person. In this section, we demonstrate, with an example, how to do unsupervised/lexicon-based emotion analysis with R.

3.3.1 Rationale of Unsupervised/Lexicon-Based Emotion Analysis

As explained in the previous section, while sentiment analysis usually reports on the tendency of positivity and negativity (and sometimes of neutrality) in a text, emotion analysis measures a number of emotional tendencies of a text, such as "joy," "sadness," "surprise," or "anger" (Ekman, 1999; Mohammad et al., 2015; Ren & Quan, 2012). Since most emotions are expressed in emotional words and phrases, it is possible and efficient to measure the emotions of a text based on a lexicon of emotions (Mohammad & Turney, 2010, 2013). Hence, researchers have developed lexicons of emotions to help facilitate the measurement of emotions, such as the the WordNet Affect Lexicon (Strapparava & Valitutti, 2004) and NRC Word-Emotion Association Lexicon (Mohammad & Turney, 2010, 2013). For example, the NRC emotion lexicon provides not only two polarity sentiments in words such as "negative" and "positive" as we examined in the previous section, but also eight different emotions: "anger," "anticipation," "disgust," "fear," "joy," "sadness," "surprise," and "trust." It is important to note that each emotion may be expressed by different words and a given word may convey different emotions in different linguistic contexts as will be shown in the next section.

3.3.2 Doing Unsupervised/Lexicon-Based Emotion Analysis with R

In this section, we provide an example of how to do unsupervised/lexicon-based emotion analysis with R. We will also use the `sentimentr` package (Rinker, 2018) for the experiment in this section since this package includes functions that help us efficiently and easily measure the emotions of a text, based on the NRC emotion lexicon (Mohammad & Turney, 2010, 2013). The data we use for the experiment is still the open dataset of Twitter US Airline Sentiment that we used in the previous two demonstrations.

Similar to what we did before, we first load the R packages that we need for the experiment (Code 3.28).

Code 3.28

```
library("dplyr")
library("readr")
library("sentimentr")
library("corrplot")
library("ggplot2")
library("tidyr")
library("aod")
```

Then, we read in the dataset and select the columns of the tweet texts and filter out the rows or cases that were manually tagged as "neutral" (Code 3.29). The read-in dataset is now stored in a data frame named df.

Code 3.29

```
> path <- "D:/"

> data <- read_csv(paste0(path, "airline_tweets.csv"))

> #select the columns: tweets and sentiments
> df <- data %>%
  select(airline_sentiment = airline_sentiment,
  text = text) %>%
  filter(airline_sentiment != "neutral")
```

Then, as an example, we measure the emotions of a sentence, specifically, those of the second tweet text in the df data frame. The tagging process is very straightforward. That is, we tag the emotions of the tweet text using the emotion_by() function. The function works primarily based on the NRC emotion lexicon (Mohammad & Turney, 2010, 2013). The results show that the tweet text contains all eight emotions included in the NRC emotion lexicon. For instance, it obtains a value of 0.47 for the emotion of "anger," 0.24 for that of "anticipation," and 0.18 for that of "disgust" (Code 3.30). To help the reader better understand how positive and negative tweets look, we have provided in Figures 3.3a and 3.3b the most positive and most negative reviews based on the emotion values received.

Code 3.30

```
> # tag a sentence
> mytext <- df$text[2]
> mytext
[1] "@VirginAmerica it's really aggressive to blast obnox-
ious \"entertainment\" in your guests' faces & they have
little recourse"
> emotion_by(mytext)
element_id emotion_type word_count emotion_count sd
ave_ emotion
 1: 1 anger 17 8 NA 0.4705882
 2: 1 anticipation 17 4 NA 0.2352941
 3: 1 disgust 17 3 NA 0.1764706
 4: 1 fear 17 5 NA 0.2941176
 5: 1 joy 17 4 NA 0.2352941
 6: 1 sadness 17 3 NA 0.1764706
 7: 1 surprise 17 7 NA 0.4117647
 8: 1 trust 17 4 NA 0.2352941
 9: 1 anger_negated 17 0 NA 0.0000000
10: 1 anticipation_negated 17 0 NA 0.0000000
11: 1 disgust_negated 17 0 NA 0.0000000
12: 1 fear_negated 17 0 NA 0.0000000
13: 1 joy_negated 17 0 NA 0.0000000
14: 1 sadness_negated 17 0 NA 0.0000000
15: 1 surprise_negated 17 0 NA 0.0000000
16: 1 trust_negated 17 0 NA 0.0000000
```

We may wonder why the tweet text also takes on emotions such as "anger," "anticipation," "joy," and "trust," particularly when the emotion is negative from the perspective of sentiment. Then, we can check out the emotion words that are responsible for the given emotions with the extract_emotion_terms() function. The results show that words such as "aggressive," "blast," and "obnoxious" are responsible for the emotion "anger," and the word "entertainment" accounts for emotions such as "anticipation," "joy," and "trust" as well as part of "surprise" (see Code 3.31 in which the tweet itself was bolded and Table 3.5 which provides simplified and clearer results shown in Code 3.31 in which the results were not lined up in a clear fashion).

ID	Emotions	Values	Reviews
1	Anger (min)	0	I saw this movie when I was about 12 when it came out. I recall the scariest scene was the big bird eating men danling helplessly from parachutes right out of the air. The horror. The horror. As a young kid going to these cheesy B films on Saturday afternoons, I still was tired of the formula for these monster type movies that usually included the hero, a beautiful woman who might be the daughter of a professor and a happy resolution when the monster died in the end. I didn't care much for the romantic angle as a 12 year old and the predictable plots. I love them now for the unintentional humor. But, about a year or so later, I saw Psycho when it came out and I loved that the star, Janet Leigh, was bumped off early in the film. I sat up and took notice at that point. Since screenwriters are making up the story, make it up to be as scary as possible and not from a well-worn formula. There are no rules.
2	Anger (max)	0.33	This was truly horrible. Bad acting, bad writing, bad effects, bad scripting, bad camera shots, bad filming, bad characters, bad music, bad editing, bad casting, bad storyline, bad... well, you get the idea. It was just, just... what's the word? oh yeah... BAD!
3	Anticipation (min)	0	I find it very intriguing that Lee Radziwill, Jackie Kennedy's sister and the cousin of these women, would encourage the Maysles' to make "Big Edie" and "Little Edie" the subject of a film. They certainly could be considered the "skeletons" in the family closet. The extra features on the DVD include several contemporary fashion designers crediting some of their ideas to these oddball women. I'd say that anyone interested in fashion would find the discussion by these designers fascinating (i.e. "Are they nuts? Or am I missing something?"). This movie is hard to come by. Netflix does not have it. Facets does, though.
4	Anticipation (max)	0.18	A film destined to be on late-night Tv long after the present instant "money-makers" have long been forgotten. Perhaps a little too subtle for today's youngsters, but in time they'll grow into an appreciation of this movie.
5	Disgust (min)	0	Once in a while, a movie will sweep along that stuns you, draws you in, awes you, and, in the end, leaves you with a renewed belief in the human race from the artistry form. This is not it. This is an action movie that lacks convincing action. It stinks. Rent something else.
6	Disgust (max)	0.33	The same as Review ID #2
7	Fear (min)	0	Ten minutes of people spewing gallons of pink vomit. Recurring scenes of enormous piles of dog excrement-need one say more???
8	Fear (max)	0.33	The same as Review ID #2

Figure 3.3a Most positive and most negative reviews based on emotion values for *anger, anticipation, disgust,* and *fear*

Code 3.31

```
> extract_emotion_terms(mytext)
  element_id sentence_id anger anticipation disgust
1: 1 1 aggressive,blast,obnoxious entertainment obnoxious
  fear joy sadness surprise trust
1: aggressive,blast entertainment obnoxious blast,enter-
tainment entertainment
```

```
sentence
1: @VirginAmerica it's really aggressive to blast obnoxious
"entertainment" in your guests' faces &amp; they have little
recourse
```

Next, let us measure the emotions of the first six tweet texts. We use the head() function to extract the first six tweet texts and store them in the variable df_head (Code 3.32). In the results of the glimpse() function, the variable is a data frame which contains six rows and two columns ("airline_sentiment," i.e., the manually tagged sentiments, and "text," i.e., the tweet texts).

ID	Emotions	Values	Reviews
9	Joy (min)	0	A brutally straightforward tale of murder and capital punishment by the state. So painfully slow and accurate in the description of capital punishment (from the preparation of the gallow to the victim p***ing in his own pants before dying) it has the power to change your mind about death penalty. The Whole Dekalog originated from this story: the Dekalog screenwriter was the powerless lawyer unsuccessfully trying to defend and then console the accused.
10	Joy (max)	0.22	real love. true love. mad love. beautifull love. ugly love. dirty love. sad love. happy love. silly love. smart love. gorgeous love. dumb love. love love love. minnie moore understand that what she really needs is a man trust her, trust her and love her madly. of course when this man comes along... she tries to run away but seymour, wonderful seymour, he trusts her, he believes in her so he is going to fight for her against her. i want to be like seymour moskowitz. i want to be that kind of man. a man willing to love without been afraid to fail but willing to fail. that's a kind of hero. tha's my kind of hero... and minnie moore is my kind of woman. long live cassavetes and all his lovely bunch!
11	Sadness (min)	0	Ming The Merciless does a little Bardwork and a movie most foul!
12	Sadness (max)	0.33	The same as Review ID #2
13	Surprise (min)	0	The same as Review ID #2
14	Surprise (max)	0.16	Hello again, I have to comment on this wonderful, exciting, and believable tale of romance and intrigue. The music in wonderful and memorable. Very good colorful movie. Another movie I liked as well later on was High Society with Bing Crosby. Wonderful music. Thanks for listening, Florence Forrester-Stockton, Reno, Nevada
15	Trust (min)	0	Comment this movie is impossible. Is terrible, very improbable, bad interpretation e direction. Not look!!!!!
16	Trust (max)	0.17	Wonderful movie. Adult content. Lots of erotic scenes puls excellent music and dance scene. My wife and I absolutely loved this movie and wish they'd make more like it.

Figure 3.3b Most positive and most negative reviews based on emotion values for *joy, sadness, surprise,* and *trust*

Table 3.5 Simplified Results for Code 3.31

Emotion	Words Tagged for the Emotion
anger	aggressive, blast, obnoxious
anticipation	entertainment
disgust	obnoxious
fear	aggressive, blast
joy	entertainment
sadness	obnoxious
surprise	blast, entertainment
trust	entertainment

Code 3.32

```
> # tag the first six tweets
> df_head <- head(df)

> glimpse(df_head)
Rows: 6
Columns: 2
$ airline_sentiment <chr> "positive", "negative", "nega-
tive", "negative", "positive", ...
$ text <chr> "@VirginAmerica plus you've added commercials to
the experie...
```

Then, we use the emotion_by() function to measure the emotions of the texts (Code 3.33). The results of the glimpse() function indicate that the resulting data frame of emotion analysis contains 96 rows (16 emotion rows for each of the six tweet texts, i.e., 16 x 6 = 96, see the next code snippet for details) and six columns.

Code 3.33

```
> df_head_emotions <- emotion_by(df_head)
> glimpse(df_head_emotions)
Rows: 96
Columns: 6
$ element_id <int> 1, 1, 1, ...
$ emotion_type <fct> anger, anticipation, disgust...
```

```
$ word_count <int> 9, 9, 9, ...
$ emotion_count <int> 0, 0, 0, ...
$ sd <dbl> 0, 0, 0, ...
$ ave_emotion <dbl> 0.00000000, 0.00000000, 0.00000000, ...
```

Let us remove the sd variable in the resulting data frame and take a look at the data frame (Code 3.34). It is obvious that the emotion_by() function returns, for each sentence or text, not only the emotion values or valences of the eight emotions that the NRC emotion lexicon (Mohammad & Turney, 2010, 2013) provides, but also the emotion values of their corresponding negated forms, though in the example sentences the values of negated forms are zero, that is, no negation occurred in the data.

Code 3.34

```
> # remove the sd variable
> df_head_emotions <- df_head_emotions %>%
+ select(-sd)
> df_head_emotions
  element_id emotion_type word_count emotion_count ave_
emotion
  1: 1 anger 9 0 0.00000000
  2: 1 anticipation 9 0 0.00000000
...
95: 6 surprise_negated 9 0 0.00000000
96: 6 trust_negated 9 0 0.00000000
  element_id emotion_type word_count emotion_count
ave_emotion
```

Now, we add the information of the manually tagged sentiments and the tweet texts to the resulting data frame. Since such information is stored in the df_head data frame, we can simply concatenate or combine the df_head and the df_head_emotions data frames to complete the task. We may use the left_join() function to concatenate two or more data frames by a certain column, such as the tweet text id. Hence, before the concatenation, we need first add a column to the df_head data frame for the tweet text id (Code 3.35). From the results of the glimpse() function, it is clear that a new column entitled "element_id" has been added to the df_head column.

Code 3.35

```
> # add the original sentiments and tweet texts
> # first, add element_id
> df_head <- df_head %>%
+ mutate(element_id = 1:length(df_head$text))
> glimpse(df_head)
Rows: 6
Columns: 3
$ airline_sentiment <chr> "positive", "negative",
"negative", "negative", "positive", ...
$ text <chr> "@VirginAmerica plus you've added commercials to
the experie...
$ element_id <int> 1, 2, 3, 4, 5, 6
```

After the variable or column of the tweet ids is prepared, we can now use the
left_join() function to combine the df_head and the df_head_
emotions data frames (Code 3.36). The results show that the resulting data
frame df_head_emotions2 now contains seven columns, with variables or
columns, such as the manually tagged sentiments and the tweet texts that were
added to the data frame df_head_emotions.

Code 3.36

```
> # add the original sentiments and tweet texts
>
> df_head_emotions2 <- left_join(df_head_emotions, df_head,
+ by = "element_id")
> glimpse(df_head_emotions2)
Rows: 96
Columns: 7
$ element_id <int> 1, 1, 1, ...
$ emotion_type <fct> anger, anticipation, ...
$ word_count <int> 9, 9, 9, ...
$ emotion_count <int> 0, 0, 0, ...
$ ave_emotion <dbl> 0.00000000, 0.00000000, 0.00000000, ...
$ airline_sentiment <chr> "positive", "positive",
"positive", ...
$ text <chr> "@VirginAmerica plus you've added commercials to
the experie...
```

Now, we examine the emotions of all the tweet texts, also with the emotion_by() function (Code 3.37).

Code 3.37

```
> # tag all the tweets
> df_all_emotions <- emotion_by(df$text)
```

In addition, if we want to add the information of the manually tagged sentiments and the tweet texts to the resulting data frame, we should concatenate the data frames of df_all and df_all_emotions. As we did for the first six tweet texts, we first add a column of tweet ids to the df_all data frame and remove sd from df_all_emotions (Code 3.38).

Code 3.38

```
> # add the original sentiments and tweet texts
> # first add element_id

> df_all <- df %>%
+ mutate(element_id = 1:length(df$text))

> # remove sd
> df_all_emotions <- df_all_emotions %>%
+ select(-sd)
```

Then, we combine the two data frames with the left_join() function (Code 3.39). The results show that the data frame now contains 184,656 rows (11,541 tweet texts x 16 emotions = 184,656 rows) and seven columns, with the variables of the manually tagged sentiments and the tweet texts added.

Code 3.39

```
> df_all_emotions2 <-
+ left_join(df_all_emotions, df_all,
+ by = "element_id")

> glimpse(df_all_emotions2)
Rows: 184,656
Columns: 7
```

```
$ element_id <int> 1, 1, 1, ...
$ emotion_type <fct> anger, anger_negated, anticipation, di
...
$ word_count <int> 9, 9, 9, ...
$ emotion_count <int> 0, 0, 0, ...
$ ave_emotion <dbl> 0.00000000, 0.00000000, 0.00000000, ...
$ airline_sentiment <chr> "positive", "positive",
"positive", ...
$ text <chr> "@VirginAmerica plus you've added commercials to
the experie ...
```

We can now use the write_csv() function to save the resulting data frame for future use (Code 3.40).

Code 3.40

```
> write_csv(df_all_emotions2, paste0(path,
"airline_emotions_lexicon_results.csv"))
```

Of course, we can examine the features of the tweets based on the automatically tagged emotions. For example, we can check out the tweets of maximum emotion values on "anger" (see Code 3.41). A total of four tweet texts are extracted, all with an "anger" value at 0.33.

Code 3.41

```
> df_all_emotions2 %>%
+ filter(emotion_type == "anger") %>%
+ filter(ave_emotion == max(ave_emotion))

  element_id emotion_type word_count emotion_count ave_
emotion airline_sentiment
1: 1741 anger 3 1 0.3333333 negative
2: 4172 anger 3 1 0.3333333 negative
3: 6897 anger 3 1 0.3333333 negative
4: 8405 anger 6 2 0.3333333 negative
  text
1: @united you're terrible.
2: @SouthwestAir horrible flight!
3: @USAirways terrible service
4: @USAirways what is the damn delay????
```

Table 3.6 Results of the lexicon-based emotion analysis

Corpus size	14,640 tweets
Manually annotated negative tweets	9,178
Manually annotated positive tweets	2,363
Manually annotated neutral tweets (excluded in the lexicon-based analysis)	3,099
Lexicon used	NRC emotion lexicon
Number of emotion words in the lexicon	13,901
Emotions examined	"anger," "anticipation," "disgust," "fear," "joy," "sadness," "surprise," "trust"
Emotion values/valences range	−1 to +1
"anger" values/valences > = 0.10	232
"anticipation" values/valences > = 0.10	450
"disgust" values/valences > = 0.10	191
"fear" values/valences > = 0.10	246
"joy" values/valences > = 0.10	360
"sadness" values/valences > = 0.10	346
"surprise" values/valences > = 0.10	146
"trust" values/valences > = 0.10	1,289

In addition, we can view the tweet texts with the maximum valence of "anticipation" (Code 3.42). The script returns two tweet texts both with the "anticipation" value at 0.5.

Code 3.42

```
> df_all_emotions2 %>%

+ filter(emotion_type == "anticipation") %>%

+ filter(ave_emotion == max(ave_emotion))

   element_id emotion_type word_count emotion_count ave_
emotion airline_sentiment
1: 5190 anticipation 2 1 0.5 positive
2: 6390 anticipation 4 2 0.5 positive
   text
1: @SouthwestAir finally!
2: @JetBlue good luck. Thanks.
```

Now we have measured the emotions of the tweet texts and obtained the eight emotion values in terms of "anticipation," "joy," etc., as well as the manually tagged sentiments such as "positive" and "negative." The results for the entire corpus are summarized in Table 3.6. This information will help us better understand the comparison of the relationships between the values of the different emotions and between the emotion values and the sentiments of the tweet texts.

Regarding the relationships between the values of the different emotions, we will first perform pairwise correlation tests among the emotion values and then conduct a logistic regression test to ascertain if any of the emotion values that we have obtained from the emotion analysis could predict the manually tagged sentiments as follows. We perform a logistic regression test here because the emotion values are continuous variables (that is, variables in numbers) and the manually tagged sentiments are of a binomial variable (that is, a variable of dichotomy in terms of "positive" and "negative"). In this logistic regression test, the manually tagged sentiments are the dependent or predicted variable and the emotion values are the independent or predictor variables.

For both the pairwise correlation and the logistic regression tests, the "wide data" format is necessary in R. That is, all the variables, either independent or dependent, should be in a column as a variable. For example, the values of the eight emotions should be in eight columns as eight variables. However, the df_all_emotions2 data frame that we previously obtained is in the "long data" format, particularly of the emotion_type column that includes the sixteen resulting emotion types (see Code 3.36). Hence, the first thing that we should do is to convert the data from the "long data" format to the "wide data" format. In Code 3.43, we select four columns (i.e., "element_id," "emotion_type," "ave_emotion," and "airline_sentiment") from the df_all_emotions2 data frame and store them in a new data frame named df_all_emotions3.

Code 3.43

```
> # preparing data format for pair-wise correlation and
logistic regression modelling
> # long data format to wide data format

> df_all_emotions3 <- df_all_emotions2 %>%
+ select(element_id, emotion_type, ave_emotion,
airline_ sentiment)
```

```
> glimpse(df_all_emotions3)
Rows: 184,656
Columns: 4
$ element_id <int> 1, 1, 1, ...
$ emotion_type <fct> anger, anger_negated, anticipation,
antici...
$ ave_emotion <dbl> 0.00000000, 0.00000000, 0.00000000,
0.0000...
$ airline_sentiment <chr> "positive", "positive",
"positive", "posit...
```

Then, we convert the "long data" format into the "wide format" with the spread() function (Code 3.44). From the results of glimpse(), we can see that in the converted "wide" data frame, sixteen new columns containing the emotion values have been added.

Code 3.44

```
> df_all_emotions_wide <- spread(df_all_emotions3,
emotion_type, ave_emotion)

> glimpse(df_all_emotions_wide)
Rows: 11,541
Columns: 18
$ element_id <int> 1, 2, 3, ...
$ airline_sentiment <chr> "positive", "negative", "nega-
tive", "ne...
$ anger <dbl> 0.00000000, 0.17647059, 0.10000000, 0.0...
$ anger_negated <dbl> 0, 0, 0, ...
$ anticipation <dbl> 0.00000000, 0.05882353, 0.00000000,
0.0...
...
$ surprise <dbl> 0.00000000, 0.11764706, 0.00000000, ...
$ surprise_negated <dbl> 0, 0, 0, ...
$ trust <dbl> 0.00000000, 0.05882353, 0.00000000, 0.0...
$ trust_negated <dbl> 0.00000000, 0.00000000, 0.0...
```

We then can perform the pairwise correlation tests among the emotion values based on the converted "wide" format of data. We do it with the cor() function which returns a correlation matrix of Pearson's r values between all the sixteen emotion values (Code 3.45).

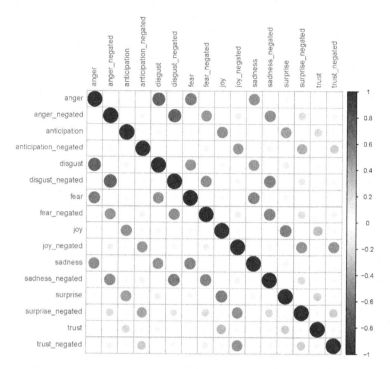

Figure 3.4 Pairwise correlations between the emotion values

Code 3.45

```
> # pair-wise correlation
> correlations <- cor(df_all_emotions_wide[, 3:18])

> correlations
  anger anger_negated anticipation anticipation_negated
anger 1.000000000 0.0045972930 0.019224141-0.011994683
anger_negated 0.004597293 1.0000000000-0.011812532
0.089071464
anticipation 0.019224141-0.0118125321 1.000000000-
0.021824247
anticipation_negated -0.011994683 0.0890714643-
0.021824247 1.000000000
disgust 0.721536097-0.0098617498 0.081668021-0.025419415
...
trust 0.271902480-3.094268e-02 1.00000000-0.062661730
```

```
trust_negated -0.032092303 2.806917e-01-0.06266173
1.000000000
```

We can also plot a correlation graph with the `corrplot()` function (Code 3.46, Figure 3.4). The graph visualizes the correlations among the emotion values, with larger circles and darker colours demonstrating stronger correlations between the variables.

Code 3.46

```
> corrplot(correlations, method="circle")
```

Now, we can start fitting the binomial logistic regression model. For logistic regression fitting, the dependent variable should be of "factor" type. Hence, we first convert the `airline_sentiment` variable into "factor" with the `as.factor()` function (Code 3.47).

Code 3.47

```
> # fitting the first Logistics Regression model
> df_all_emotions_wide$airline_sentiment <-
as.factor(df_all_emotions_wide$airline_sentiment)
```

Then, we fit the logistic regression model with the `glm()` function (Code 3.48). Note that the first parameter of the function is the formula of the regression, with the dependent or predicted variable on the left side of the tilde (~) and the independent or predictor variables on the right side of the tilde. Also, the parameter `family = binomial` means this is to fit a binomial logistic regression model.

Code 3.48

```
> logit_model <- glm(airline_sentiment ~
+ anger + anger_negated +
+ anticipation + anticipation_negated +
+ disgust + disgust_negated +
+ fear + fear_negated +
+ joy + joy_negated +
+ sadness + sadness_negated +
+ surprise + surprise_negated +
```

```
+ trust + trust_negated,
+ data = df_all_emotions_wide,
+ family = binomial)
```

We can take a look at the results of the model with the summary() function (Code 3.49). The results show that of the sixteen predictor variables, nine ones are significant (with an asterisk after the p. value).

Code 3.49

```
> summary(logit_model)
Call:
glm(formula = airline_sentiment ~ anger + anger_negated +
anticipation +
    anticipation_negated + disgust + disgust_negated + fear +
    fear_negated + joy + joy_negated + sadness + sadness_negated +
    surprise + surprise_negated + trust + trust_negated, family =
binomial,
    data = df_all_emotions_wide)
Deviance Residuals:
Min 1Q Median 3Q Max
-4.4537-0.7027-0.5542-0.2161 3.3715
Coefficients:
Estimate Std. Error z value Pr(>|z|)
(Intercept) -1.27278 0.03414-37.286 < 2e-16 ***
anger -8.78204 1.79412-4.895 9.84e-07 ***
anger_negated -4.59432 6.49199-0.708 0.479137
anticipation -5.08006 0.90892-5.589 2.28e-08 ***
anticipation_negated -3.59832 2.79775-1.286 0.198392
disgust -6.81760 1.83389-3.718 0.000201 ***
disgust_negated -12.46809 8.42592-1.480 0.138945
fear -2.17901 1.38827-1.570 0.116511
fear_negated -15.16341 4.94228-3.068 0.002154 **
joy 20.46116 1.03991 19.676 < 2e-16 ***
joy_negated 10.93602 5.43049 2.014 0.044029 *
sadness -13.08046 1.28559-10.175 < 2e-16 ***
sadness_negated 1.25768 3.89033 0.323 0.746480
surprise 0.11584 1.33146 0.087 0.930671
surprise_negated -12.77134 6.75275-1.891 0.058587 .
trust 1.80401 0.43657 4.132 3.59e-05 ***
trust_negated -31.65969 3.71165-8.530 < 2e-16 ***
```

```
‾
Signif. codes: 0 '***' 0.001 '**' 0.01 '*' 0.05 '.' 0.1 ' ' 1

(Dispersion parameter for binomial family taken to be 1)

   Null deviance: 11701 on 11540 degrees of freedom
Residual deviance: 10295 on 11524 degrees of freedom
AIC: 10329

Number of Fisher Scoring iterations: 6
```

Since some of the predictor variables are not significant, we fit the model for the second time, excluding the insignificant variables (Code 3.50). Concerning the results of the second modelling, eight of the nine predictor variables are significant.

Code 3.50

```
> # fitting the second Logistics Regression model
> logit_model2 <- glm(airline_sentiment ~
+ anger +
+ anticipation +
+ disgust +
+ fear_negated +
+ joy + joy_negated +
+ sadness +
+ trust + trust_negated,
+ data = df_all_emotions_wide,
+ family = binomial)

> summary(logit_model2)

Call:
glm(formula = airline_sentiment ~ anger + anticipation +
disgust +
   fear_negated + joy + joy_negated + sadness + trust +
trust_negated,
   family = binomial, data = df_all_emotions_wide)

Deviance Residuals:
  Min 1Q Median 3Q Max
  -4.4404-0.6975-0.5535-0.2250 3.3747

Coefficients:
  Estimate Std. Error z value Pr(>|z|)
(Intercept) -1.28965 0.03357-38.421 < 2e-16 ***
```

```
anger -9.51325 1.74304-5.458 4.82e-08 ***
anticipation -5.05739 0.87179-5.801 6.58e-09 ***
disgust -6.93097 1.81802-3.812 0.000138 ***
fear_negated -19.67692 4.39049-4.482 7.40e-06 ***
joy 20.44739 0.95594 21.390 < 2e-16 ***
joy_negated 5.08290 4.97192 1.022 0.306629
sadness -13.65273 1.22874-11.111 < 2e-16 ***
trust 1.84882 0.43532 4.247 2.17e-05 ***
trust_negated -32.31323 3.70426-8.723 < 2e-16 ***
-
Signif. codes: 0 '***' 0.001 '**' 0.01 '*' 0.05 '.' 0.1 ' ' 1
(Dispersion parameter for binomial family taken to be 1)

    Null deviance: 11701 on 11540 degrees of freedom
Residual deviance: 10310 on 11531 degrees of freedom
AIC: 10330

Number of Fisher Scoring iterations: 6
```

Thus, we should fit the logistic regression model for the third time, excluding the insignificant variable (i.e., joy_negated, Code 3.51). Now, all the eight predictors are significant. Let us explain the model with the results of two predictors. The results show that for each unit change in the predictor variable "anger," the log odds of the dependent or predicted variable "positive" (versus negative) decrease by 9.52. In addition, for every unit change in the predictor variable "joy," the log odds of the dependent or predicted variable "positive" (versus negative) increase by 20.45.

Code 3.51

```
> # fitting the third Logistics Regression model
> logit_model3 <- glm(airline_sentiment ~
+ anger +
+ anticipation +
+ disgust +
+ fear_negated +
+ joy +
+ sadness +
+ trust + trust_negated,
+ data = df_all_emotions_wide,
+ family = binomial)
>
> summary(logit_model3)
```

```
Call:
glm(formula = airline_sentiment ~ anger + anticipation +
  disgust +
fear_negated + joy + sadness + trust + trust_negated, family =
binomial,
  data = df_all_emotions_wide)

Deviance Residuals:
Min 1Q Median 3Q Max
-4.4398-0.6979-0.5526-0.2248 3.3745

Coefficients:
Estimate Std. Error z value Pr(>|z|)
(Intercept) -1.28831 0.03354-38.414 < 2e-16 ***
anger -9.51675 1.74295-5.460 4.76e-08 ***
anticipation -5.06090 0.87176-5.805 6.42e-09 ***
disgust -6.92412 1.81787-3.809 0.00014 ***
fear_negated -19.33956 4.37151-4.424 9.69e-06 ***
joy 20.44666 0.95594 21.389 < 2e-16 ***
sadness -13.65999 1.22857-11.119 < 2e-16 ***
trust 1.84188 0.43526 4.232 2.32e-05 ***
trust_negated -30.64033 3.25150-9.423 < 2e-16 ***
-
Signif. codes: 0 '***' 0.001 '**' 0.01 '*' 0.05 '.' 0.1 ' ' 1
(Dispersion parameter for binomial family taken to be 1)

  Null deviance: 11701 on 11540 degrees of freedom
Residual deviance: 10311 on 11532 degrees of freedom
AIC: 10329

Number of Fisher Scoring iterations: 6
```

We can also check the confident intervals with profiled log-likelihood of the coefficients of the significant variables using the confint() function or the confident intervals with standard errors of the coefficients using the confint. default() function (Code 3.52).

Code 3.52

```
> ## Confident intervals with profiled log-likelihood
> confint(logit_model3)
Waiting for profiling to be done ...
  2.5 % 97.5 %
```

```
(Intercept) -1.354343-1.222870
anger -12.991481-6.156799
anticipation -6.787965-3.370236
disgust -10.479210-3.367535
fear_negated -28.497829-11.297439
joy 18.590333 22.338138
sadness -16.104038-11.286096
trust 0.982820 2.690433
trust_negated -37.363636-24.587592

> ## Confident intervals with standard errors
> confint.default(logit_model3)
  2.5 % 97.5 %
(Intercept) -1.3540370-1.222574
anger -12.9328555-6.100636
anticipation -6.7695161-3.352285
disgust -10.4870809-3.361161
fear_negated -27.9075560-10.771560
joy 18.5730498 22.320269
sadness -16.0679437-11.252032
trust 0.9887879 2.694967
trust_negated -37.0131611-24.267508
```

Last, we can also explain the coefficients of the predictors as odds ratios. We convert the coefficients into odds ratios by exponentiating the coefficients (Code 3.53). Based on the results, when the predictor "anger" changes a unit, the odds of "positive" (versus "negative") increase by a factor of 0.000074 (i.e., a very slim chance to increase). In addition, when the predictor "trust" changes a unit, the odds of "positive" (versus "negative") increase by a factor of 6.31 (i.e., a large chance to increase).

Code 3.53

```
> ## odds ratios and 95% CI

> exp(cbind(odds_ratio = coef(logit_model3),
  confint(logit_model3)))

Waiting for profiling to be done ...
  odds_ratio 2.5 % 97.5 %
(Intercept) 2.757377e-01 2.581169e-01 2.943840e-01
anger 7.360881e-05 2.279667e-06 2.119026e-03
anticipation 6.339848e-03 1.127261e-03 3.438152e-02
```

```
disgust 9.837673e-04 2.811491e-05 3.447450e-02
fear_negated 3.989667e-09 4.202910e-13 1.240465e-05
joy 7.583529e+08 1.184892e+08 5.027246e+09
sadness 1.168268e-06 1.014157e-07 1.254616e-05
trust 6.308372e+00 2.671981e+00 1.473805e+01
trust_negated 4.932554e-14 5.931697e-17 2.097705e-11
```

3.4 Summary

In this section, we have demonstrated step-by-step how to do sentiment analysis using R with three examples involving the same data (tweets about airlines and their services): one example used a supervised machine-learning method, one used an unsupervised/lexicon-based machine-learning method, and an additional one used an unsupervised/lexicon-based method but for performing emotion analysis, rather than sentiment analysis. The detailed demonstrations should help the reader not only understand but be able to perform all the necessary procedures involved in conducting sentiment analysis using R and the R packages available for such analysis.

4 Case Study 1: A Diachronic Analysis of Sentiments and Emotions in the State of the Union Addresses

This section provides a case study using an unsupervised/lexicon-based method to perform a diachronic sentiment analysis and an emotion analysis of the *State of the Union addresses* (hereafter SOTUs) given by 45 US presidents spanning 230 years (beginning from the first address delivered by President George Washington in 1790 to the most recent one given by President Donald Trump in 2020). The purpose of this case study is to help the reader see how a complete unsupervised/lexicon-based sentiment and emotion analysis study is conducted, particularly how the results of such a study are reported, explored, and discussed. We will first provide some background information including the rationale for this study followed by a brief description of the method. Then, we will report and discuss in detail the results and their implications.

4.1 Background

4.1.1 The SOTUs and Reasons for a Diachronic Sentiment/Emotion Analysis of Them

To begin with, the SOTU is an annual event where the US president delivers a formal speech to a joint session of the US Congress usually at the beginning of each calendar year. Mandated by the US Constitution as specified in Article II, Section 3, Clause 1, the annual SOTU typically includes a report on the conditions of the nation (especially the economic and financial conditions) as well as the policy agenda and national priorities his/her administration has for the coming year to help keep the nation strong or make it stronger (Shogan, 2016). Although the SOTU is delivered to Congress, it also has "the American public" as its other key audience because the president needs the public's support to implement the agendas proposed in the address (Shogan, 2016, p. 14). Because of their unique significant role in American politics, SOTUs are arguably some of the most important public documents about the United States and the directions it has been going since its founding. Second, all the SOTUs perform the same function, are similar in format and style (i.e., they are all formal speeches), and cover essentially the same issues. In other words, they are of the same genre, making them especially suitable for a diachronic comparative study (Lei & Wen, 2019; Savoy, 2015). Third, transcripts of the yearly SOTUs have been kept in the Congress's Art, History & Archives under the heading "State of the Union Address" (https://history.house.gov/Institution/SOTU) and hence they constitute systematically collected historical documents for diachronic analysis. In fact, although there has not been any sentiment analysis of SOTUs, there have been a few diachronic studies quite recently (e.g., Lei & Wen, 2019; Savoy, 2015; Shogan, 2016) about some other aspects of these important speeches, to which we now turn.

4.1.2 Existing Research on SOTUs

Of the recent diachronic studies on SOTUs, Shogan's (2016) updated Congressional Research Service report on the tradition, function, and policy implications of the SOTU provides valuable information about the common rhetoric sequence, major recurring themes (e.g., bipartisanship and optimism), and the policy impact of the SOTUs as well as some changes that have taken place in length, format, and style since 1790. Savoy's (2015) study focused on the clustering and authorship attribution concerning the SOTUs from 1790 to 2014, involving a total of 224 speeches given by 41 presidents. Using a principal component analysis (PCA) involving the part-of-speech (POS) frequencies, Savoy (2015) was able to find that since President Franklin Roosevelt's 1934 SOTU, "each president tends to own a distinctive style whereas previous presidents tend usually to share some stylistic aspects with others" (p. 1645). Regarding noticeable rhetoric styles in the SOTUs, Desjardins's (2018) informal analysis finds that "strong" is the word that almost all the presidents used in describing the state of the nation although there have been a few exceptions. For example, President Ford in his 1975 SOTU said "the State of the Union is not good" due to the fact that the country had just gone through the Watergate scandal and finished the Vietnam War without a victory. Lei and Wen's (2019) study examined the syntactic complexity of the language, in terms of the dependency distance, in SOTUs over the last 227 years. The study found that the language in the SOTUs has become less complex in syntax. These studies have clearly enhanced our understanding about the SOTUs. However, as noted above, none of them was a sentiment analysis.

4.1.3 Research Purposes and Questions

Against the backdrop presented here, this case study aims to explore whether sentiments and emotions in the SOTUs have changed over the past 230 years. The specific purpose of this case study is two-fold: first, to demonstrate how to do lexicon-based sentiment and emotion analysis from a diachronic perspective; and second, to explore and discuss any diachronic changes in sentiment and emotion shown in the SOTUs, especially those possible changes during important historic events in the United States. The following are the research questions that this case study intends to answer.

Research question 1: What is the nature of sentiments in the SOTUs? Is there any change of sentiments across the past 230 years?

Research question 2: What is the nature of emotions in the SOTUs? Is there any change of emotions across the past 230 years?

In the following sections, we will first describe the methods used in this case study, and then present our findings. We will also offer a brief discussion on the findings and their implications.

4.2 Methods

4.2.1 Data

The data used in this study is the corpus of the SOTUs downloaded from the American Presidency Project (http://presidency.proxied.lsit.ucsb.edu) developed and maintained by the University of California, Santa Barbara. The data contains a total of 230 addresses by all the 43 presidents, starting from the very first one by President George Washington in 1790 to the most recent one in the corpus given by President Donald Trump in 2020.

4.2.2 Data Processing and Analysis

We used the unsupervised/lexicon-based approach to measure the sentiments and emotions of the addresses. The procedures for data processing are described as follows.

For research question 1, we first measured the sentiment values of each piece of the SOTUs. Second, we fit a simple linear regression model to test whether the sentiment has experienced any significant change across the examined 230 years. Last, we examined the years with the highest and the lowest sentiment values. For research question 2, we first computed the values of the eight emotions for each SOTU. Second, we performed an ANOVA test to ascertain if the eight emotions were significantly different. Third, we fit simple linear regression models to determine whether the emotions have experienced any significant change across the 230 years being studied. Last, we examined the years with the highest and the lowest emotion values.

We used the R package `sentimentr` (Rinker, 2018) for both the sentiment analysis and the emotion analysis. In addition, we used R for all the other statistical analyses, such as the simple linear regression tests and the ANOVA test.

4.3 Results and Discussion

4.3.1 Sentiment Analysis

The sentiment values of the SOTUs across 230 years are illustrated in Figure 4.1. The result of the simple linear regression model showed that the sentiment values of SOTUs had experienced no significant diachronic change ($F(1, 228)$ = 0.1639, Multiple R-squared = 0.0007182, Adjusted R-squared = –0.003665, p = 0.686). That is, the sentiments in SOTUs are fairly stable and have not experienced any significant change across the 230 years with the mean sentiment value being 0.1544 – a positive value since, as mentioned earlier, a positive value indicates a positive sentence/text (whose sentiment value is sentence based) and a negative value suggests a negative one. However, it is important to note while all the 230 SOTUs registered a positive score, the difference across them is very large with the lowest being 0.0195 (President Franklin D. Roosevelt's 1942 SOTU) and the highest being 0.389 (President Washington's 1790). This means that the sentiment of the latter SOTU is twenty times that of the former SOTU. What lowers the sentiment of a SOTU is mainly the number of its paragraphs/sentences that received a negative sentiment value. Generally, with other factors being constant, the larger the number of negative paragraphs/sentences a SOTU has, the lower its sentiment score will be. This overall positive result of the SOTUs indirectly supports previous research findings that the SOTUs had showcased a few recurring themes with optimism being one of them (Shogan, 2016) and maintained a positive tone as evidenced by the use of the word "strong" by almost every president in almost every speech (Desjardins, 2018).

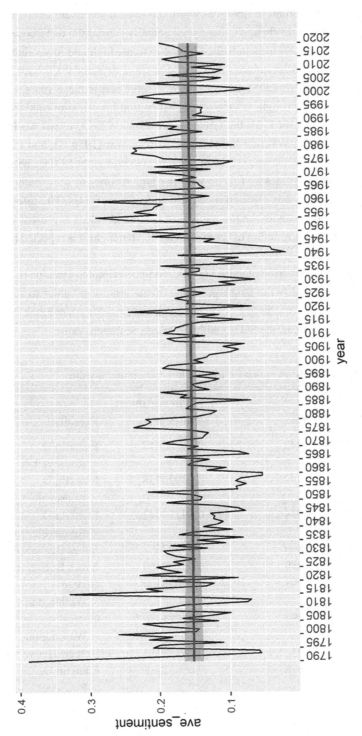

Figure 4.1 Sentiments of the *State of the Union Addresses* across 230 years (the line in the middle of the plot is the regression line)

However, it is important to note that while the overall sentiment over the 230 years remained little changed, there were actually substantial differences among some of the SOTUs as indicated by the extreme high and low values shown in Figure 4.1. Such substantial variations are understandable because the conditions of the United States were not the same across these years. In fact, the nation went through, among other challenging historical events, the American Civil War (1861–5), the Great Depression (1929–33), two world wars (WWI, 1914–18; WWII, 1939–45), the Korean War (1950–3), and the Vietnam War (1969–73). It would thus be of interest to look at the SOTUs with the lowest sentiment values and those with the highest ones to see whether important historical events affected the sentiments of the SOTUs. The information of the addresses with the top ten lowest sentiment values is presented in Table 4.1 and the information of those with the top ten highest is reported in Table 4.2.

Before a general discussion of these SOTUs, it will be helpful to examine two paragraphs that exemplify the language with extreme sentiment values to see how such language looks. The first is a paragraph taken from President Frank D. Roosevelt's 1942 address, the SOTU with the lowest sentiment value:

Table 4.1 Addresses with top ten lowest sentiment values

ID	Year	Mean sentiment values	President
1	1942	0.01945618	Franklin D. Roosevelt
2	1943	0.03920738	Franklin D. Roosevelt
3	1944	0.04224042	Franklin D. Roosevelt
4	1860	0.05397657	James Buchanan
5	1859	0.05409369	James Buchanan
6	1793	0.05622400	George Washington
7	1794	0.05944276	George Washington
8	1932	0.06373613	Herbert Hoover
9	1938	0.06822888	Franklin D. Roosevelt
10	1922	0.06860750	Warren G. Harding

Table 4.2 Addresses with top ten most positive sentiments

ID	Year	Mean sentiment	President
1	1790	0.3890208	George Washington
2	1815	0.3295840	James Madison
3	1961	0.2914743	Dwight D. Eisenhower
4	1955	0.2893600	Dwight D. Eisenhower
5	1791	0.2893520	George Washington
6	1800	0.2597287	John Adams
7	1920	0.2433117	Woodrow Wilson
8	1954	0.2415427	Dwight D. Eisenhower
9	1979	0.2376256	Jimmy Carter
10	1990	0.2365575	George H. Bush

*We must **guard** against **divisions** among ourselves and among all the other United Nations. We must be particularly <u>vigilant</u> against racial **discrimination** in any of its **ugly** forms. Hitler will try again to breed **mistrust** and **suspicion** between one individual and another, one group and another, one race and another, one Government and another. He will try to use the same technique of **falsehood** and **rumor-mongering** with which he divided France from Britain. He is trying to do this with us even now. But he will find a <u>unity</u> of will and purpose against him, which will <u>persevere</u> until the **destruction** of all his **black designs** upon the <u>freedom</u> and <u>safety</u> of the people of the world.*

In this paragraph, Roosevelt was discussing the serious dangers that the United States and its allies were facing from Hitler (and his Nazi government) and the actions and resolves needed to defeat Hitler's evil intentions. The paragraph received a negative score of −0.554, the second highest negative score among all the paragraphs in the speech. It should be noted that although the absolute negative value of this as well as the other negative paragraphs was not extreme, the SOTU received the lowest sentiment value because a very large number of its paragraphs/sentences were negative. A main reason for this paragraph's high negative score is Roosevelt's use of many negative words (marked in bold, ten in total) to portray the dangers presented by Hitler's evil designs. The number of these words doubled that of the positive words (underlined). It should also be noted, though, that although the word "destruction" was negative, the phrase "destruction of all his black designs" was actually positive.

The second example is taken from President Washington's 1790 address, the first ever SOTU and also the one boasting the highest sentiment value.

> *In pursuing the various and weighty business of the present session I indulge the fullest persuasion that your consultation will be equally marked with wisdom and animated by the love of your country. In whatever belongs to my duty you shall have all the cooperation which an undiminished zeal for its welfare can inspire. It will be happy for us both, and our best reward, if, by a successful administration of our respective trusts, we can make the established Government more and more instrumental in promoting the good of our fellow citizens, and more and more the object of their attachment and confidence.*

In this paragraph, Washington was expressing a highly positive expectation of a very cooperative and successful work relationship with the members of Congress as evidenced by the numerous positive words (all underlined). These positive words helped the paragraph earn a high positive sentiment score of 0.9857, the second highest positive value in the speech.

Let us now turn to the SOTUs with the lowest sentiment values. Most of them occurred during very trying times that the United States was undergoing. For example, President Frank D. Roosevelt's 1942 SOTU occurred just a couple of months after the horrific December 7, 1941, Japanese attack on Pearl Harbour, arguably the worst foreign attack that the nation had ever experienced until then. The second and third lowest ranked SOTUs were also President Franklin D. Roosevelt's delivered in 1943 and 1944, respectively, when the United States was in the thick of protracted brutal battles against the Axis forces. The fourth and fifth lowest ranked were President Buchanan's SOTUs in 1860 and 1859, a time of turmoil with growing divisions over slavery that would soon lead to the Civil War in 1861.

The sixth and seventh lowest were the SOTUs given by President Washington in 1793 and 1794, which might look surprising, at least on the surface. However, a scrutiny of Washington's presidency in those two years and the years before them reveals that he and his administration were confronted with at least two serious challenges. One was the grain farmers' rebellion against the new alcohol tax that led to what is known as the Whiskey Rebellion in 1794, which his administration had to resort to both federal and state armed forces to quell (Kohn, 1972). The other was the prolonged unsuccessful fight with the Northwest Native American tribes, which were instigated by and allied with British troops. The troops Washington dispatched for the fight suffered several serious defeats before finally winning the fight in August 1794.

The eighth lowest one was delivered by President Hoover in 1932, a year in the heat of the Great Depression. The ninth lowest was given by F. D. Roosevelt in 1938 and the tenth lowest was delivered by Harding in 1922. While the low sentiment of President Harding's 1922 SOTU was likely caused by the fact that the country had been undergoing a post-WWI deflationary depression since 1920, the low sentiment of Roosevelt's 1938 SOTU appeared to have resulted from the tumultuous international events (such as Japan's invasion of China in 1937) before WWII and the challenges at home as shown in the following paragraphs from this speech.

> But in a world of high tension and disorder, in a world where stable civiliza-
> tion is actually threatened, it becomes the responsibility of each nation which
> strives for peace at home and peace with and among others to be strong
> enough to assure the observance of those fundamentals of peaceful solution
> of conflicts which are the only ultimate basis for orderly existence.
>
> That, I assert, is not an inherent right of citizenship. For if a man farms his
> land to the waste of the soil or the trees, he destroys not only his own assets
> but the Nation's assets as well. Or if by his methods he makes himself, year
> after year, a financial hazard of the community and the government, he
> becomes not only a social problem but an economic menace. The day has
> gone by when it could be claimed that government has no interest in such ill-
> considered practices and no right through representative methods to stop
> them.

Both paragraphs received a negative score. In the first paragraph, Roosevelt was discussing international conflicts and arguing for the need for the United States to strive to stop such conflicts because at that time there was a strong non-intervention mood in the United States. In the second paragraph, he was defending his policy of government controlling excessive surpluses in farm production.

In short, it seems that adverse historical events might have been a main reason for the low sentiments of these SOTUs. This may be supported by the fact that President Roosevelt, who had four of his SOTUs in the top ten negative ones, actually made a quite positive SOTU in 1934 (his second year in office) with a sentiment score of 0.1601, which is higher than the mean and eight times higher than that of his 1942 SOTU. In this SOTU, Roosevelt celebrated what he had accomplished since he took office because the US economy had indeed begun to recover from the Great Depression with the implementations of his new policies (Eggertsson, 2008). The following paragraph from the speech helps illustrate his positive sentiment:

> It is to the eternal <u>credit</u> of the American people that this tremendous
> readjustment of our national life is being <u>accomplished peacefully</u>, without

serious dislocation, with only a minimum of injustice and with a <u>great</u>, <u>willing</u>
<u>spirit</u> of <u>cooperation</u> throughout the country.

In this paragraph, Roosevelt, as a very polished politician, was giving credit
to the American people for the accomplishments achieved since he took office.
The use of positive words underlined in the paragraph helps it earn a high
positive score of 0.6654. This paragraph contrasts sharply with the very negative paragraph from his 1942 SOTU cited previously.

However, it is simultaneously important to note that a few SOTUs from years
that had just experienced tragic events (e.g., 2002 after the 9/11 attack in 2001 and
1951 after the outbreak of the Korean War) failed to make the list of SOTUs with
the ten lowest sentiment values. These puzzling findings would suggest that there
might be other influencing factors than historical events in determining the sentiment of a SOTU, such as the president's personality and/or speech style, an issue
we will explore in Section 4.3.2 concerning the results of the emotion analysis.

Now, let us move on to the ten SOTUs with the highest positive sentiment
values (reported in Table 4.2). President George Washington's 1790 SOTU, the
first ever and the shortest of all the SOTUs, boasted the highest positive value.
Its high positive value might have resulted from President Washington's inten-
tion to set a very positive tone for this new but important recurring form of
speech to Congress and the American public. President James Madison's 1815
SOTU attained second place. A possible reason for its high positive value might
have been the signing of the Treaty of Ghent in the previous year (1814) because
the treaty officially ended the war between the newly founded nation and
Britain. President Dwight D. Eisenhower's 1961, 1955, and 1954 SOTUs
were the third, fourth, and eighth most positive. It is necessary to point out
that his 1961 SOTU was his last one given on January 12 and there was another
SOTU that year delivered by the incoming president, John F. Kennedy, less than
twenty days later on January 30. In other words, there were two SOTUs that
year. Double SOTUs in one year happened three times in history when both the
outgoing and incoming presidents each gave a SOTU: 1953 (Truman and
Eisenhower), 1961 (Eisenhower and Kennedy), and 1981 (Carter and
Reagan). We considered and calculated only the outgoing presidents' addresses
since it was very rare for the incoming president to give a SOTU address in the
first year of office particularly when the outgoing presidents had already given
one. Considering that there were over 230 SOTUs and that there did not appear
to have been extraordinary achievements in 1961, 1955, and 1954, the fact that
Eisenhower had three of his SOTUs ranked in the top ten most positive ones
might be because he was a very optimistic person and/or had a highly positive
speech style. Of course, the high positivity of his 1954 and 1955 speeches could

also have been motivated by or reflected the peaceful time after the Korean War ended in 1953 and the continued baby boom since the end of WWII.

President Washington's fifth-ranked 1791 SOTU might have owed its high positive sentiment to the fact that it was the second SOTU, which followed his first and the most positive SOTU in 1790 (i.e., the high positivity in his first SOTU might have spilled over to his second one). On the other hand, President John Adams's sixth-ranked 1800 SOTU might have been positively influenced by the upcoming signing of the Convention of 1800 that year, which ended the conflict between the United States and France. Similarly, President Woodrow Wilson's seventh-ranked 1920 SOTU might have inherited the positive spirit from the ending of WWI just over a year ago. Of the ninth- and tenth-highest positively ranked SOTUs, while the reason for the high positive sentiment in President George Bush's 1990 speech might have been the imminent end of the Cold War, there does not appear to be any clear reason for the high positivity in President Jimmy Carter's 1979 SOTU, for in that year the United States was in a very poor economic condition with abnormally high inflation and low growth due largely to the high rise of oil prices (*Federal Reserve Bank of Minneapolis Quarterly Review*, 1980). In fact, Carter lost to Ronald Reagan in the presidential election the very next year. However, Carter was very positive about the economy in this SOTU as he declared in the speech, "Our economy offers greater prosperity for more of our people than ever before." He was obviously overly optimistic.

Carter's case shows again that there might be other reasons influencing the sentiment of the SOTUs than the actual conditions or historical events, such as personality. One more point worth noting is the great shift in sentiment between President Washington's highly positive 1790 and 1791 SOTUs (ranked first and fifth most positive) and his very negative 1793 and 1794 ones (ranked sixth and seventh most negative). The prolonged wars with Britain and the Northwest Native American tribes, and the Whiskey Rebellion seemed to have really dented Washington and his administration's positive sentiment shown in 1790 and 1791. If this was indeed the case, then it, along with the contrast between President Roosevelt's 1934 and 1942 SOTUs, would suggest that historical events might be a much more significant factor affecting the sentiment of a given SOTU than the personality traits of the presidents.

4.3.2 Emotion Analysis

The emotion values of the SOTUs across the 230 years examined are illustrated in Figures 4.2a and 4.2b, and their descriptive statistics are presented in Table 4.3.

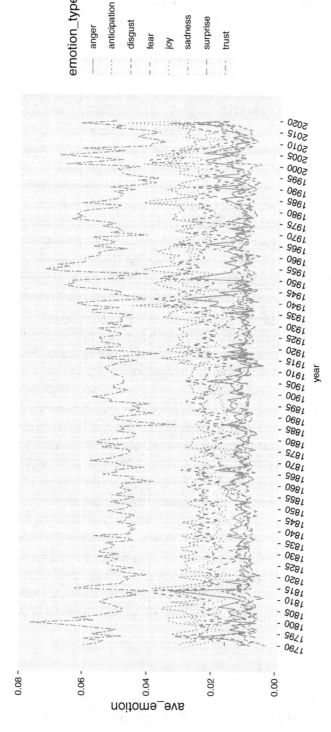

Figure 4.2a Emotions of the *State of the Union Addresses* across 230 years

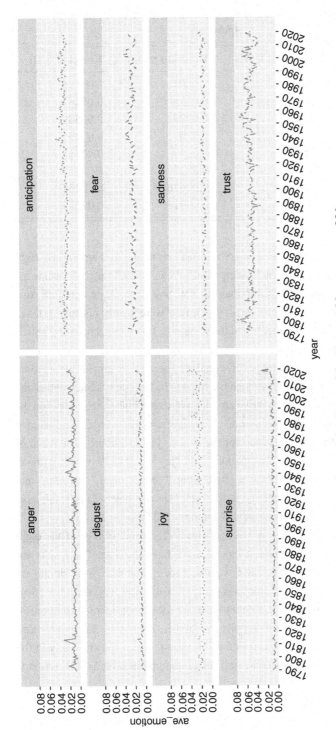

Figure 4.2b Emotions of the *State of the Union Addresses* across 230 years

Table 4.3 Descriptive statistics of the eight emotions in the *State of the Union Addresses*

ID	Emotion types	Emotion means	Emotion S.D.
1	trust	0.0503	0.00695
2	anticipation	0.0278	0.00467
3	fear	0.0220	0.00509
4	joy	0.0209	0.00494
5	anger	0.0130	0.00411
6	sadness	0.0122	0.00272
7	surprise	0.00930	0.00264
8	disgust	0.00914	0.00223

The results show that the mean value of "trust" ranks the first among the eight emotions, followed in order by "anticipation," "fear," "joy," "anger," "sadness," "surprise," and "disgust." It is important to note that of the eight emotions, two were apparently positive ("trust" and "joy"), four were clearly negative ("fear," "anger," sadness," and "disgust"), and the remaining two seemed neutral ("anticipation" and "surprise"). However, of these two seemingly neutral ones, "anticipation" appears to possess a strong positive tendency because as humans we are more likely to anticipate positive than negative things. To help determine whether the values of the positive or the negative emotion words are higher, we computed the mean values for both the positive and negative emotion words. We included "anticipation" in the positive group for the reasons just mentioned. The mean of the positive group ("trust," "anticipation," and "joy") is 0.0330, which is much higher than the 0.0141 mean of the negative group ("fear," "anger," "sadness," and "disgust"), indeed, the former more than doubles the latter. This result also demonstrates the overall positive sentiment in the SOTUs.

Then, to test whether there is any significant diachronic change of the eight emotions, simple linear regression models were fit to the data. The results are reported in Table 4.4. Based on the p. values, it seems that there were significant diachronic changes for all the emotions except "trust." However, since the effect sizes (the estimates of beta) are all minuscule, we should consider the emotions in the SOTUs to have remained largely stable (i.e., they have not experienced significant diachronic changes across the 230 years), just as shown clearly in the results of the simple linear regression tests of the sentiments in the SOTUs reported earlier.

Last, we extracted the six SOTUs with the highest emotion values in each of the top four emotions (i.e., "trust," "anticipation," "fear," and "joy"). The results are reported in Tables 4.5, 4.6, 4.7, and 4.8.

Table 4.4 Results of simple linear regression models of the eight emotions

ID	Emotion types	F values	D.F.	Multiple R^2	Multiple R^2	p.	Estimates of Beta
1	trust	0.068	(1, 228)	0.0002994	-0.004085	0.7941	1.795e-06
2	anticipation	38.5	(1, 228)	0.1445	0.1407	2.555e-09	2.654e-05
3	fear	8.57	(1, 228)	0.03623	0.032	0.003764	1.446e-05
4	joy	64.59	(1, 228)	0.2208	0.2173	4.95e-14	3.470e-05
5	anger	7.858	(1, 228)	0.03332	0.02908	0.005495	1.120e-05
6	sadness	30.35	(1, 228)	0.1175	0.1136	9.71e-08	1.393e-05
7	surprise	51.28	(1, 228)	0.1836	0.18	1.094e-11	1.688e-05
8	disgust	6.357	(1, 228)	0.02713	0.02286	0.01237	5.491e-06

Table 4.5 Addresses with the highest *trust* values

ID	Year	Presidents	Trust
1	1800	John Adams	0.07641921
2	1955	Dwight D. Eisenhower	0.07177099
3	1957	Dwight D. Eisenhower	0.06793087
4	2005	George W. Bush	0.06723186
5	1799	John Adams	0.06578073
6	1948	Harry S. Truman	0.06569201

Table 4.6 Addresses with the highest *anticipation* values

ID	Year	Presidents	Anticipation
1	1939	Franklin D. Roosevelt	0.04464993
2	1984	Ronald Reagan	0.04137377
3	1955	Dwight D. Eisenhower	0.04136420
4	2001	George W. Bush	0.04131477
5	1985	Ronald Reagan	0.03930337
6	1815	James Madison	0.03815580

Table 4.7 Addresses with the highest *fear* values

ID	Year	Presidents	Fear
1	2002	George W. Bush	0.03986451
2	2003	George W. Bush	0.03951763
3	1942	Franklin D. Roosevelt	0.03860346
4	1813	James Madison	0.03801349
5	1814	James Madison	0.03782506
6	1951	Harry S. Truman	0.03611457

Table 4.8 Addresses with highest *joy* values

ID	Year	Presidents	Joy
1	2019	Donald J. Trump	0.04629630
2	1984	Ronald Reagan	0.03896365
3	2001	George W. Bush	0.03515179
4	2005	George W. Bush	0.03292587
5	1965	Lyndon B. Johnson	0.03233775
6	1950	Harry S. Truman	0.03219550

In terms of "trust," two presidents (Adams and Eisenhower) each had two SOTUs that boasted very high values. "Trust" is often used in America to mean trust in God (e.g., the American motto "In God we trust"). It is thus no accident at all these presidents whose SOTUs boasted high trust values were well-known staunch religious believers. Adams famously declared that Christian tenets were "bearers of freedom, a cause that still had a holy urgency" (Brookhiser, 2002, p. 13). For Eisenhower, it is reported that when he was a child, his parents designated specific times at breakfast and dinner for daily family Bible reading (Ambrose, 1983). President George W. Bush is a well-known born-again Christian and viewed as the most religious president for generations (Keller, 2003). A look at the SOTUs by the presidents in question showed that the presidents, with the exception of Adams, indeed made mentions of trust in God.

Concerning "anticipation," which often involves the presentation or projection of great things to come, it is not surprising that Roosevelt, famous for his effective communication skills in modern politics, had his 1939 SOTU ranked with the highest and Reagan, nicknamed "the Great Communicator" for making inspiring speeches (Cooper, 2008), had his 1984 and 1985 SOTUs ranked with the second and fifth highest values in this emotion category. However, Eisenhower, George W. Bush, and Madison, who were perhaps not known as great speakers, each had one SOTU ranked high in "anticipation" values. This could suggest that a president may be able to create great expectations mainly with superior legislative and presidential agendas.

Regarding "fear," the SOTUs with the highest values in this category appeared to be mostly the ones delivered during war times. For example, Bush's 2002 and 2003 speeches were given during the war on terrorism right after the horrendous September 11 terrorist attack. Roosevelt's 1942 SOTU was given right after the Pearl Harbour attack and after the United States had officially entered WWII. Truman's 1951 speech was delivered the year after the Korean War had broken out. Once again, the result here indicates how historical events might have affected the sentiment of the SOTUs.

As for "joy," which should correlate positively with "anticipation," it is not surprising, again, that Reagan's 1984 speech (which ranked with the second highest value in "anticipation") was ranked with the second highest value in this category as well and the 2019 SOTU by Trump, who is famous for giving rousing, sensational, or grandiose speeches, came in first. It is also important to point out that again, as in the case with the "anticipation" emotion category, several presidents not particularly known for their speaking skills, such as George W. Bush, Johnson, and Truman, each also had one or two SOTUs boast very high "joy" values. This fact perhaps can help affirm again that a president can convey and inspire joy with great agendas and policies. Furthermore, the overall results reported here demonstrate clearly how historical events and a president's personality can significantly shape the sentiments of SOTUs.

4.4 Summary

This section has presented a case study of sentiment and emotion analysis of the SOTUs over 230 years. It has shown the important steps involved in the data analysis and illustrated how the results are analyzed, reported, and discussed. The unsupervised/lexicon-based method that we used has identified the key sentiments and emotions and helped to show how such sentiments and emotions have remained stable and quite positive over the years. The results of our sentiment and emotion analysis provide support for the findings of previous non-sentiment studies that the SOTUs have stayed generally very positive, evidencing the value and validity of sentiment and emotion analysis. In addition, our analysis and discussion have shown how historical events as well as other factors such as a president's speech style and personality might have affected the sentiment and emotion values of the SOTUs.

5 Case Study 2: A Sentiment and Emotion Analysis of Movie Reviews

This section offers a case study using a supervised machine-learning approach in the sentiment analysis of 50,000 movie reviews taken from the Internet Movie Database (IMDb), along with an unsupervised/lexicon-based aspect-level emotion analysis of these reviews. The purpose is to allow the reader to see how the supervised machine-learning procedures introduced in Section 3.1 are applied to both document-level and aspect-level sentiment analyses and understand the challenges involved.

5.1 Background

Movies are a very popular form of entertainment for the public. Many new movies are released each year and numerous movie reviews are written about these movies. Usually, each movie receives many reviews, especially in this internet age. However, different reviews of the same movie may vary, sometimes greatly, in their evaluations. Hence, it would be of interest and importance to learn the overall opinion or sentiment of the reviews of a given movie. Sentiment analysis of movie reviews can provide this useful information systematically. Below we briefly review existing research on sentiment analysis of movie reviews and the major challenges involved.

5.1.1 Existing Research

The past two decades have witnessed many studies on this topic, especially those about how to make sentiment analyses of movie reviews more accurate and effective (e.g., Ali, Abd El Hamid & Youssif, 2019; Pang, Lee & Vaithyanathan, 2002; Parkhe & Biswas, 2016; Singh et al., 2013; Thet, Na & Khoo, 2010, Turney, 2002).

Pang et al. (2002) and Turney (2002) were among the early studies on sentiment analysis of reviews with the former pioneering in supervised machine-learning methods and the latter experimenting with unsupervised methods. Their studies have led to and inspired recent work exploring new techniques. For example, Ali et al. (2019) innovated with a deep-learning method that incorporated and combined deep-learning networks, such as Multilayer Perception and Convolutional Neural networks, in the sentiment analysis of 50,000 movie reviews from the IMDb. Quite a few of the existing studies explored how sentiment analysis of movie reviews should be at the aspect level focusing on the key aspects of a movie, such as acting and script/story, and how to conduct such analysis (e.g., Parkhe & Biswas, 2016; Singh et al., 2013; Thet et al., 2010). We will briefly review these studies in the next section because there are various challenges in conducting aspect-level analysis.

5.1.2 Challenges in Aspect-Level Analysis

While there are various challenging issues, we focus on two here: (1) what aspects to include in an aspect-level analysis and (2) how to deal with sentiments in movie reviews that are not about the movies being reviewed but about the characters and other issues.

Concerning the first issue, Thet et al. (2010, p. 827) proposed six major aspects: "overall," "cast," "director," "story," "scene," and "music," with each including some sub-aspects. For example, "cast" encompasses "act, acting, actress … " (Thet et al., 2010, p. 827). On the other hand, Singh et al. (2013, p. 7) considered eleven major aspects, such as "award, editing, dialogues, cinematography, choreograph, script/story, music, film-making …." Obviously, there is substantial overlap, especially considering the fact that often different terms are used to refer to the same aspect, e.g., Thet et al.'s (2010) "cast" actually also refers to acting with the latter being a sub-aspect of the former. Furthermore, Parkhe and Biswas (2016) examined which aspects were the driving factors for the sentiment of a movie across different movie genres and found that driving aspects varied across genres. Also, for each genre, there were usually three driving aspects and some of them overlap across genres, such as "acting," "directing," and "screenplay" (i.e., script/story).

Concerning the second challenging issue, Thet et al. (2010) noted that movie reviewers often use negative words to describe the characters (e.g., evil man) and/or the storyline (e.g., tragic ending), but these negative words and expressions were not about the quality of a movie. In other words, these negative words differ from those negative ones about the quality of a movie. However, currently, most sentiment analysis algorithms are not able to make this distinction and often include the negative words unrelated to the quality of a movie in the overall assessment of the reviews about the movie. Much work is thus needed to address this problem.

5.1.3 Purposes of the Present Study

As stated, this study aims to demonstrate how to conduct a supervised machine-learning sentiment analysis (polarity terms of negativity versus positivity) of movie reviews. It uses high-frequency words of the movie reviews being studied as the classification features and fits a Naïve Bayes model to classify and predict the sentiments of the reviews. The study will also evaluate the model based on the prediction accuracy of the model. Because this supervised analysis method, like most sentiment analysis algorithms, assesses movie reviews only as negative or positive, we will also conduct an unsupervised/lexicon-based emotion study of the reviews using the NRC emotion lexicon (Mohammad & Turney, 2010, 2013) introduced in Section 3.3.1. The lexicon covers eight major emotions. This emotion analysis will be aided by an aspect-level analysis of the strongest emotions so as to provide a more detailed descriptive picture of the sentiments and emotions in the movie reviews. It should be noted that our aspect-level analysis will be done manually rather than with aspect-level

Table 5.1 Statistics of the movie review dataset

	Positive reviews	Negative reviews
Number of reviews	25,000	25,000
Number of words	5,908,854	5,828,670
Average number of words per review	236.35	233.15

supervised learning methods as done in Thet et al. (2010) and Parkhe and Biswas (2016) for the following two reasons. First, aspect-level learning methods have not been thoroughly developed and sophisticated aspect-specific lexicons are scarce. As a result, R packages, such as `syuzhet` (Jockers, 2017a) and `sentimentr` (Rinker, 2018) that we are using in this Element, have not embedded any aspect-specific lexicons. Second, supervised/lexicon-based learning methods involving aspect analysis, such as those used in Thet et al. (2010) and Parkhe and Biswas (2016), are rather complex and beyond the purview and space of this Element.

5.2 Methods

5.2.1 The Data

The data used in the study were the Large Movie Review Dataset v1.0 constructed by Maas et al. (2011). The data contained 50,000 IMDb movie reviews, of which half are tagged as positive reviews and the other half as negative reviews manually based on the developers' judgment. Since all the reviews in the dataset were tagged with their sentiments (negative versus positive polarity), it is possible for us to use the dataset for our experiment on the supervised machine-learning sentiment analysis. The dataset may be downloaded from http://ai.stanford.edu/~amaas/data/sentiment/aclImdb_v1.tar.gz or www.kaggle.com/lakshmi25npathi/imdb-dataset-of-50 k-movie-reviews. The statistics of the dataset are summarized in Table 5.1.

5.2.2 The Procedures of Data Processing

The procedures of data processing in the experiment include the following. First, the `tm` package is used to convert the review texts into a corpus and the corpus data are then cleaned, such as changing all words into lower case and removing punctuation, stop words, numbers, and white spaces since these are not relevant features for the sentiment classification tasks.

Second, a Document Term Matrix (DTM) is developed with the `DocumentTermMatrix()` function embedded in the `tm` package. The DTM is a matrix of words in each of the review text and their corresponding frequency in each text. Then, words with a total frequency of more than ten are chosen as the feature words. It should be noted that the frequencies of these words are treated simply as a binary factor of "Yes" (when the frequency is larger than ten in our specific case) or "No" (when the frequency equals ten or less here). This is because it is the occurrence or nonoccurrence of these words, rather than their frequency, that is used as the classification feature related to this issue in a review text. Hence, the information of these words and their presence or absence in a review will be used as the features for the classification of the sentiments (see Section 3.1 for more discussions on the selection of feature words).

Third, we split the dataset into two parts – the training set and the testing set. Of the dataset, 75 percent (37,500 review texts) were randomly chosen and used as the training set and 25 percent (12,500 review texts) were used as the testing set.

Fourth, a Naïve Bayes model is trained and the model is used to predict the sentiments of review texts in the testing set. In addition, a confusion matrix is built and the accuracy of the model is calculated to evaluate the Naïve Bayes model.

For the unsupervised/lexicon-based emotion analysis, we use the `sentimentr` package to perform the data analysis using the procedures as described in Section 3.3. Review texts with top emotion values are then analyzed manually according to the relevant aspects of the movies. This manual lexicon-based analysis is used here because there are no appropriate trained data of movie reviews available for machine-learning emotion analysis and no aspect-specific lexicons embedded in R packages as noted before.

The reasons for the lack of such data and lexicons are threefold. First, unlike sentiment analysis which often has only one dimension (i.e., positivity vs negativity), emotion analysis covers as many as eight dimensions or types (as shown in Section 3.3.1), which makes it much more complicated and labour-intensive to do manual emotion tagging. Second, as will be shown with examples in Section 5.3.2, classifying emotion is challenging because some emotion types may overlap (e.g., *anger* and *disgust*), which may be conveyed by the same words simultaneously). Third, as in the case of sentiment analysis where it is difficult to differentiate words that describe the characters or stories of the movie from those that evaluate the movie itself, emotion words describing characters or stories may be mistakenly included in the emotion analysis of the review (examples will be given in the following).

5.3 Results and Discussion

5.3.1 Supervised Machine-Learning Sentiment Analysis of Movie Reviews

As discussed previously, high-frequency words in the review texts are used as the feature words in the experiment (i.e., they play an important role in the classification of the sentiments of the texts). The word cloud of the high-frequency words was plotted and illustrated in Figure 5.1.

The confusion matrix of the supervised learning sentiment analysis is presented in Table 5.2. The results show that of the 6,225 negative review texts, 5,305 were correctly tagged as "negative" and 920 were incorrectly tagged as "positive" by the Naïve Bayes model. In addition, of the 6,275 positive review texts, 5,258 texts were correctly tagged as "positive," and 1,017 were incorrectly tagged as "negative" by the Naïve Bayes model. The overall accuracy of the Naïve Bayes model was 84.50 percent (95 percent CI: 83.86 percent, 85.13 percent).

While an overall accuracy of 84.50 percent is considered satisfactory and comparable to those of existing such analysis (e.g., Maas et al. 2011), still 15.50 percent (i.e., nearly 2,000 out of the 12,500 reviews) were incorrectly tagged. This fact indicates that there are substantial challenges involved in determining the sentiments of movie reviews because some reviews are not crystal clear in their overall evaluation and sometimes human tagging can be incorrect as can be seen in the following two reviews from the corpus. The first was tagged positive

Figure 5.1 Word cloud of high-frequency words in the movie reviews

Table 5.2 Confusion matrix of the supervised learning sentiment analysis

Prediction	negative	positive
negative	5,305	920
positive	1,017	5,258

manually but negative by our machine-learning method; the second one was tagged negative manually but positive by the machine-learning method.

> *This is probably the first entry in the "Lance O'Leary/Nurse Keat" detective series; in subsequent O'Leary films, he was played by much younger actors than Guy Kibbee. A group of relatives (all played by well-known character actors) gathers in an old house (on a rainy nite, of course!) to speak to a wealthy relative, who goes into a coma. While they wait for him to recover, all sorts of mysterious goings-on happen, including a couple of murders. A creepy film; worth seeing!*
>
> *When I saw the trailers I just HAD to see the film. And when I had, I kinda had a feeling that felt like unsatisfied. It was a great movie, don't get me wrong, but I think the great parts were already in the trailers, if you catch my drift. It went very fast and it rolled on, so I was never bored, and I enjoyed watching it. The humor was absolutely great. My first contact with a sloth (.. or something like it).*

The difficulty with determining the positive/negative polarity of the first review lies in the fact that whereas it contains several negative words about the plot, such as *mysterious, murders,* and *creepy,* it ends with a positive evaluative phrase containing an exclamation mark *worth seeing!* Here, the positive human tagging should be considered correct based on the positive concluding evaluative phrase; the negative machine-learning classification seemed to be erroneously influenced by those negative words about the story. The difficulty with the second review involves seemly self-contradictory evaluations, such as *felt like unsatisfied* vs. *a great movie, enjoyed watching it,* and *humor was absolutely great.* Taken as a whole, the review should be considered positive. In other words, the human tagging was incorrect this time and it appeared to have been based mostly on the *felt like unsatisfied* phrase without taking all the positive evaluative phrases into consideration. Fortunately, the machine-learning tagging was correct.

Furthermore, the challenges negative/positive binary sentiment analysis faces also betrays the simplicity of such a method and the limitations of its application. Without providing a numerical value for the polarity sentiments, the method could not show how negative or positive a given review was and which reviews were the most negative or positive. Fortunately, what is missing

Table 5.3 Descriptive statistics of emotions in the
movie reviews

Emotion type	Mean	S.D.
trust	0.0283	0.0159
anticipation	0.0247	0.0144
joy	0.0234	0.0158
fear	0.0207	0.0155
sadness	0.0184	0.0138
anger	0.0160	0.0135
surprise	0.0141	0.0110
disgust	0.0138	0.0131

in the results of the supervised learning method might be compensated some-what by the results of our unsupervised/lexicon-based emotion study involving a manual aspect-level analysis reported in the next section.

5.3.2 Aspect-Level Emotion Analysis of Movie Reviews

The descriptive results of the emotion analysis are summarized in Table 5.3. The eight emotion types are listed in order of their mean values from high to low. Given that the reviews are actually evenly divided in sentiment – 50 percent negative and 50 percent positive based on Maas et al.'s (2011) tagging – it is surprising that the three positive emotions ("trust," "anticipation," and "joy") boasted the highest values, all higher than those of the four negative emotions ("fear," "sadness," "anger," and "disgust"). One plausible reason for the dis-crepancy between these results and Maas et al.'s binary negative/positive results might be the difference in the classification of the sentiments and emotions. For instance, Maas et al. (2011) included other sentiment types such as "melan-choly," "ghastly," "lackluster," and "romantic." Such differences in what senti-ment/emotion words to include for analysis between different lexicons and algorithms serve as additional evidence about the complexity and challenges involved in the sentiment/emotion analysis of movie reviews.

In order to run an aspect-level analysis of the emotions, we extracted the review texts with the top five values in each of the eight emotion types. We then manually classified the aspects assessed by the reviews according to the follow-ing six aspect categories that we adopted based on a synthesis of Singh et al.'s (2013) and Thet et al.'s (2010) classification systems discussed previously: (1) overall, (2) acting/performance, (3) script/story, (4) directing, (5) cinematog-raphy, and (6) music. To help illustrate and discuss the findings, we have

Table 5.4 Reviews with top five values of *anger*

ID	Mean value	Review text	Aspect
1	0.33	This was truly horrible. Bad acting, bad writing, bad effects, bad scripting, bad camera shots, bad filming, bad characters, bad music, bad editing, bad casting, bad storyline, bad . . . well, you get the idea. It was just, just . . . what's the word? Oh yeah . . . BAD!	1) overall 2) acting/performance 3) script/story 4) directing 5) cinematography 6) music
2	0.15	Olivier Gruner stars as Jacques a foreign exchange college student who takes on and single handedly wipes out a Mexican street gang in this obnoxious and racist film which is so horrible that it's laughable. Bad acting, bad plot and bad fight choreography make Angel Town a Turkey.	1) overall 2) acting/performance 3) script/story 5) cinematography
3	0.14	This movie is so bad it's almost good. Bad story, bad acting, bad music, you name it. O.K., who are the jokers that gave this flick a '10'?	1) overall 2) acting/performance 3) script/story 5) cinematography
4	0.14	Crazy Six is torture, it must be Albert Pyun's worst film. Even Blast and Ticker are better! I can't believe how boring this film is! How this even got greenlighted? I saw this movie about 3 years ago and the only thing I remember is how bad it was. This isn't good bad movie, it is simply bad, bad, bad, bad, bad movie.1 out of 10 (½ out of *****)	1) overall 2) acting/performance

5   0.14   A brutally straightforward tale of murder and capital punishment by the state. So painfully slow and accurate in the description of capital punishment (from the preparation of the gallow to the victim p***ing in his own pants before dying) it has the power to change your mind about death penalty. The whole Dekalog originated from this story: the Dekalog screenwriter was the powerless lawyer unsuccessfully trying to defend and then console the accused.

2) acting/performance

Table 5.5 Reviews with top five values of *disgust*

ID	Mean	Review text	Aspect
6	0.33	The same as ID #1	1) overall 2) acting/performance 3) script/story 4) directing 5) cinematography 6) music
7	0.19	Acting is horrible. This film makes Fast and Furious look like an academy award winning film. They throw a few boobs and butts in there to try and keep you interested despite the EXTREMELY weak and far fetched story. There is a reason why people on the internet aren't even downloading this movie. This movie sunk like an iron turd. DO NOT waste your time renting or even downloading it. This film is and always will be a PERMA-TURD. I am now dumber for having watched it. In fact this title should be referred to as a "PERMA-TURD" from now on. Calling it a film is a travesty and insult. abhorrent, abominable, appalling, awful, beastly, cruel, detestable, disagreeable, disgusting, dreadful, eerie, execrable, fairy, fearful, frightful, ghastly, grim, grisly, gruesome, heinous, hideous, horrendous, horrid, loathsome, lousy, lurid, mean, nasty, obnoxious, offensive, repellent, repulsive, revolting, scandalous, scary, shameful, shocking, sickie, terrible, terrifying, ungodly, unholy, unkind	1) overall

8	0.16	it really is terrible, from start to finish you'll sit and watch this ridiculous idiot, thinking hes cool when he's really not, rubbish plot line, terrible acting and complete waste of time and money, do NOT bother.	1) overall 2) acting/performance 3) script/story
9	0.15	Really bad movie. Maybe the worst I've ever seen. Alien invasion, a la The Blob, without the acting. Meteorite turns beautiful woman into a host body for nasty tongue. Bad plot, bad fake tongue. Absurd comedy worth missing. Wash your hair or take out the trash.	1) overall 2) acting/performance 3) script/story
10	0.15	John Leguizamo must have been insane if he thinks this was a funny movie. I laughed more times watching Remains of the Day. Pathetic plot, unbearable acting. Horrible music – Michael Sambello IS a "Maniac."	1) overall 2) acting/performance 3) script/story 6) music

Table 5.6 Review texts and aspects with top five highest values of *joy*

ID	Mean Value	Review texts	Aspect
11	0.22	real love. true love. mad love. beautiful love. ugly love. dirty love. sad love. happy love. silly love. smart love. gorgeous love. dumb love. love love love. minnie moore understands that what she really needs is a man who trust her, trust her and love her madly. of course when this man comes along . . . she tries to run away but seymour, wonderful seymour, he trusts her, he believes in her so he is going to fight for her against her. i want to be like seymour moskowitz. i want to be that kind of man. a man willing to love without been afraid to fail but willing to fail. that's my kind of hero . . . and minnie moore is my kind of woman. long live cassavetes and all his lovely bunch!	2) acting/performance 3) script/story 4) directing
12	0.21	Wonderful movie. Adult content. Lots of erotic scenes plus excellent music and dance scenes. My wife and I absolutely loved this movie and wish they'd make more like it.	1) overall 2) acting/performance 5) cinematography 6) music
13	0.20	Great movie – especially the music – Etta James – "At Last." This speaks volumes when you have finally found that special someone.	1) overall 6) music
14	0.19	The acting is good, the action is good, and so is the plot. If you like some good, fast entertainment with an air for authentic action scenes, not the Hollywood (looks great, but is totally ridiculous) kind, you're in for a special treat. Just sit back and enjoy . . .	2) acting/performance 3) script/story 5) cinematography

15   0.18   Hello again, I have to comment on this wonderful, exciting, and believable tale of romance and intrigue. The music in wonderful and memorable. Very good colorful movie. Another movie I liked as well later on was High Society with Bing Crosby. Wonderful music. Thanks for listening. . .

1) overall
3) script/story
5) cinematography
6) music

Table 5.7 Reviews with top five values of *trust*

ID	Mean Value	Review texts	Aspect
16	0.17	The same as ID #12	1) overall 2) acting/performance 5) cinematography 6) music
17	0.17	Certainly any others I have seen pale in comparison. The series gives balanced coverage to all theatres of operation. No one country is given undue credit for the Allied victory. Laurence Olivier brings great weight and dignity to his role as narrator.	1) overall 2) acting/performance 3) script/story
18	0.17	The same as ID #14	2) acting/performance 3) script/story 5) cinematography
19	0.16	An absoloutely wonderful film that works on several levels. It's a story about a great architect, a son seeking his father, about very loving relationships, and about loss. It's also a great film about architecture. Very intelligent and very moving. A real treat.	1) overall 3) script/story
20	0.16	What a show! Lorenzo Lamas once again proves his talent as a cop who committed the worst crime a good cop can commit, by being a good cop. Then, again, he shows how sensitive a cop can be, displaying a range of emotions like no other actor can except, maybe, himself in Terminal justice. HUGE ENJOYMENT!	2) acting/performance

included the analysis results of four of the eight emotions (two positive and two negative) in Tables 5.4–5.7.

Four important points can be drawn from the results of the aspect-level emotion analysis. First, sometimes, the emotion score did not appear to be based on reviewer's evaluation of the movie but on the reviewer's description of the movie, especially its plots/stories. The review of ID #5 (the last one in the top five values of "anger") provides an excellent example about this problem. Despite registering the fifth highest "anger" value due to its description of the movie involving brutal murder and capital punishment, the review actually was quite positive about the movie as evidenced by the statements "So ... accurate in the description of capital punishment ... it has the power to change your mind about death penalty." This demonstrates again the challenge in sentiment/emotion analysis of movie reviews where descriptions may often be interpreted as evaluations. Second, some of the emotion scores did not appear to accurately reflect the intensity of the emotions. For instance, in the results concerning the "disgust" emotion category, the review with ID #7, (i.e., the review with a "disgust" score of 0.19, the second highest in this emotion category) actually used many more "disgust"-related words than the review with ID #6, which received a much higher score of .33 and ranked first in the category. In fact, this review (ID #7) literally exhausted all the "disgust"-related words by listing them in alphabetical order (likely taken from a thesaurus). This fact raises questions about the accuracy of the analysis, that is, the accuracy of the algorithms used in determining/assigning emotion values.

Third, many of the review texts were on the top five lists of several different emotions. For examples, the review (ID #1) that received the highest value in *anger* also boasted the highest value in all the other three negative emotions: *disgust, fear,* and *sadness*. As another example, two of the top five *joy* reviews were also on the top five *trust* list. These results suggest that there is significant overlap between some of the emotions, raising questions about

Table 5.8 Evaluation frequency for each aspect

Aspect	Counts
(1) overall	29
(2) acting/performance	27
(3) script/story	25
(4) cinematography	15
(5) music	13
(6) directing	9

the need to have them as separate emotion types in emotion analysis. Fourth, the number of aspects covered varied substantially across the reviews with one review (ID #1) encompassing all six aspects while a few touched on just one (typically the "overall" aspect). To understand the extent of this variation and its implications, we tabulated the number of times each aspect was evaluated. The results (reported in Table 5.8) show that three of the six aspects ("overall," "acting/performance," and "script/story") received substantially more evaluations than the other three aspects, a result that supports Parkhe and Biswas's (2016) aforementioned finding that there are usually three driving aspects for the reviews in each movie genre. This finding may suggest that aspect-level sentiment analysis may only need to focus on two or three aspects.

5.4 Summary

This section has demonstrated how to conduct a supervised machine-learning sentiment analysis of movie reviews as well as an unsupervised/lexicon-based emotion study of these reviews that involved an aspect-level analysis. Whereas the results have shown relatively satisfactory accuracy of the machine-learning method, they have also revealed the limitations of the negative/positive polarity-based analysis used in the method. Furthermore, while the aspect-level emotion analysis expanded our understanding of the movie reviews, its results, which differed noticeably from those of supervised machine-learning methods and which also exhibited questionable emotion value determinations, have also shown again the complexity and challenges inherent in the sentiment/emotion analysis of movie reviews. Obviously, a lot of improvement is still needed in this line of research.

6 Conclusion: Where We Are and Where We Are Heading

In this Element, we have discussed what sentiment analysis is, what its main applications are, how successful it has been, and what its main challenges are (Section 1), described the common methods employed in sentiment analysis (Section 2), demonstrated step-by-step procedures for conducting both supervised machine-learning and unsupervised/lexicon-based sentiment/emotion analysis with R (Section 3), and illustrated, with two case studies, how to conduct real sentiment analyses and interpret/discuss the results and their implications (Sections 4 and 5). Based on what has been presented, we briefly summarize here the current state of research on sentiment analysis (i.e., where we are), and the challenges and future directions in this line of research (i.e., where we are heading).

Our discussion in this Element has shown that sentiment analysis is growing rapidly and has been applied widely across many domains, including business/ finance, political science, and healthcare/medicine. Furthermore, sentiment analysis has achieved some success although it still faces some challenges. Regarding success, sentiment analysis studies have generally attained an accuracy range between 65 percent and 90 percent. More importantly, with advances in technology, many new innovative approaches and algorithms, especially those involving deep learning, have been developed for both unsupervised/lexicon-based and supervised machine-learning-based sentiment/emotion analyses. For example, for unsupervised/lexicon-based analysis, there are now both cross-domain (or general) lexicons and domain-specific lexicons as well as aspect-level lexicons (e.g., Hamilton et al, 2016; Singh et al., 2013). As for supervised machine-learning analysis, new algorithms incorporating various deep-learning networks are now being developed (e.g., Ali et al., 2019).

In terms of challenges, there is still room and need to enhance accuracy. Issues affecting the accuracy of sentiment analysis include the following. First, there are not enough cross-domain lexicons for unsupervised/lexicon-based studies and not enough training data sets that can be effectively applied to a wide range of domains; there are also not enough domain-specific lexicons (Zunic et al., 2020), especially those that can take into consideration cultural and language differences (Gopaldas, 2014). Another area where much more work is needed is to make our algorithms better able to consider contextual information in the determination of the sentiments of words, phrases, and sentences by integrating more "human analysis to classify sentiments according to the language context as well as interpret the valence of a sentiment from the text" (Rambocas & Pacheco, 2018, p. 159). To achieve this goal will require the incorporation of cutting-edge knowledge from disciplines other than computer science and natural language processing, such as cultural anthropology, clinical psychology, and sociology (Gopaldas, 2014).

Furthermore, although sentiment analysis has involved more languages, so far it appears to have been concentrated on English, Chinese, Arabic, and Indian languages. More work is needed in other languages. In addition, while sentiment analysis has been conducted in many different domains, it can be expected to continue expanding into new areas where no or little such research has been done.

Finally, we would like to end this Element with the note that there are a lot of potential topics for sentiment analysis in linguistics, especially applied linguistics. Although research on sentiment analysis has blossomed across many domains and disciplines, it appears that such work is only in the budding stage in linguistics/applied linguistics with only a few published sentiment studies in this area as reported in Section 1. We hope more applied/corpus linguists will seize the opportunity and embark on this promising line of research.

References

Ali, N. M., Abd El Hamid, M. M., & Youssif, A. (2019). Sentiment analysis for movies reviews dataset using deep learning models. *International Journal of Data Mining & Knowledge Management Process*, *9*(2/3), 19–27.

Ambrose, S. (1983). *Eisenhower: Soldier, general of the army, president-elect (1893–1952)*. New York: Simon & Schuster.

Antonakaki, D., Spiliotopoulos, D., Samaras, C. V., Pratikakis, P., Ioannidis, S., & Fragopoulou, P. (2017). Social media analysis during political turbulence. *PLoS ONE*, *12*(10), e0186836.

Biber, D. (2006) Stance in spoken and written university registers. *Journal of English for Academic Purposes*, *5*, 97–116.

Brookhiser, R. (2002). *America's first dynasty: The Adamses, 1735–1918*. New York: Simon & Schuster.

Cambria, E., Poria, S., Bajpai, R., & Schuller, B. (2016). SenticNet 4: A semantic resource for sentiment analysis based on conceptual primitives. In Y. Matsumoto & R. Prasad (eds.), *Proceedings of COLING 2016, the 26th international conference on computational linguistics: Technical papers* (pp. 2666–2677). Osaka, Japan.

Cao, X., Lei, L., & Wen, J. (2020). Promoting science with linguistic devices: A large-scale study of the use of positive and negative words in academic writing. *Learned Publishing*, https://doi.org/10.1002/leap.1322.

Chen, Y., & Skiena, S. (2014). Building sentiment lexicons for all major languages. In K. Toutanova & H. Wu (eds.), *Proceedings of the 52nd annual meeting of the Association for Computational Linguistics (short papers)* (pp. 383–389). Baltimore, MD.

Collins COBUILD English Dictionary. (1987). Glasgow, UK: HarperCollins.

Conrad, S., & Biber, D. (2000). Adverbial marking of stance in speech and writing. In S. Hunston & G. Thompson (eds.), *Evaluation in text: Authorial stance and the construction of discourse* (p. 56–73). Oxford: Oxford University Press.

Cooper, J. (2008). The Reagan years: The Great Communicator as diarist. *Intelligence and National Security*, *23*(6), 892–901.

D'Andrea, A., Ferri, F., Grifoni, P., & Guzzo, T. (2015). Approaches, tools and applications for sentiment analysis implementation. *International Journal of Computer Applications*, *125*(3), 26–33.

Davenport, T. H., & Harris, J. G. (2009). What people want (and how to predict it). *MIT Sloan Management Review*, *50*(2), 23–31.

Davies, M. (2008–) *The corpus of contemporary American English*. www .english-corpora.org/coca/ (last accessed April 2021).

Denecke, K., & Deng, Y. (2015). Sentiment analysis in medical settings: New opportunities and challenges. *Artificial Intelligence in Medicine*, *64*(1), 17–27.

Desjardins, L. (January 30, 2018). The word nearly every president uses to describe the state of the union. *PBS NewsHour*. www.pbs.org/newshour/ politics/the-word-nearly-every-president-uses-to-describe-the-state-of-the-union (accessed August 13, 2020).

Dipper, S. (2008). Theory-driven and corpus-driven computational linguistics, and the use of corpora. In A. Lüdeling & M. Kytö (eds). *Corpus linguistics: An international handbook* (pp. 68–96). Berlin/New York: de Gruyter.

Eggertsson, G. B. (2008). Great expectations and the end of the Depression. *American Economic Review*, *98*(4), 1476–1516.

Ekman, P. (1999). Basic emotions. In T. Dalgleish & M. J. Power (eds.), *Handbook of cognition and emotion* (pp. 45–60). Hoboken, NJ: Wiley.

Federal Reserve Bank of Minneapolis Quarterly Review, Vol. 4, No. 1 (1980). https://ideas.repec.org/s/fip/fedmqr2.html (accessed August 15, 2020).

Feldman, R. (2013). Techniques and applications for sentiment analysis. *Communication of the ACM*, *56*(4), 82–89.

Garcia, D. (2013). Sentiment during recessions. *The Journal of Finance*, *68*(3), 1267–1300.

Gayo-Avello, D. (2012a). I wanted to predict elections with Twitter and all I got was this lousy paper: A balanced survey on election prediction using Twitter data. arXiv preprint arXiv:1204.6441.

Gayo-Avello, D. (2012b). No, you cannot predict elections with Twitter. *Internet Computing, IEEE*, *16*(6), 91–94.

Giuntini, F. T., Cazzolato, M. T., dos Reis, M. d. J. D., Campbell, A. T., Traina, A. J. M., & Ueyama, J. (2020). A review on recognizing depression in social networks: Challenges and opportunities. *Journal of Ambient Intelligence and Humanized Computing*, Advance online publication. https://doi.org/10.1007/s12652-020-01726-4.

Gonçalves, P., Benevenuto, F., & Cha, M. (2013). Panas-t: A psychometric scale for measuring sentiments on twitter. arXiv preprint:1308.1857.

Gopaldas, A. (2014). Marketplace sentiments. *Journal of Consumer Research*, *41*(4), 995–1014.

Hajek, P., Olej, V., & Myskova, R. (2014). Forecasting corporate financial performance using sentiment in annual reports for stakeholders' decision-making. *Technological and Economic Development of Economy*, *20*(4), 721–738.

Hamilton, W. L., Clark, K., Leskovec, J., & Jurafsky, D. (2016). Inducing domain-specific sentiment lexicons from unlabeled corpora. In J. Su, K. Duh, & X. Carreras (eds.), *Proceedings of the conference on empirical methods in natural language processing*, (pp. 595–605). Austin, TX.

Homburg, C., Ehm, L., & Artz, M. (2015). Measuring and managing consumer sentiment in an online community environment. *Journal of Marketing Research*, *52*(5), 629–641.

Hu, Y., Hsiau, W., Shih, S., & Chen, C. (2018). Considering online consumer reviews to predict movie box-office performance between the years 2009 and 2014 in the US. *The Electronic Library 36*(6), 1010–1026.

Hu, M., & Liu, B. (2004). Mining and summarizing customer reviews. In W. Kim, R. Kohavi, J. Gehrke, & W. DuMouchel (eds.), *The 2004 ACM SIGKDD international conference* (pp. 168–177). Seattle, WA.

Hunston, S. (2011). *Corpus approaches to evaluation: Phraseology and evaluative language*. London: Routledge.

Hur, M., Kang, P., & Cho, S. (2016). Box-office forecasting based on sentiments of movie reviews and independent subspace method. *Information Sciences*, *372*, 608–624.

Ikoro, V., Sharmina, M., Malik, K., & Batista-Navarro, R. (2018). Analyzing sentiments expressed on Twitter by UK energy company consumers. In *2018 fifth international conference on social networks analysis, management and security (SNAMS 2018)*. (pp. 95–98). Valencia, Spain: IEEE. https://doi.org/10.1109/SNAMS.2018.8554619.

Jockers, M. (2017a). *Syuzhet* (Version 1.04) [Computer software]. https://github.com/mjockers/syuzhet.

Jockers, M. (2017b). *Syuzhet sentiment lexicon* [Computer software]. https://github.com/mjockers/syuzhet.

Jungherr, A., Schoen, H., Posegga, O., & Jürgens, P. (2017). Digital trace data in the study of public opinion: An indicator of attention toward politics rather than political support. *Social Science Computing*, *35*, 336–356.

Katti, R. (2016). Naïve Bayes classification for sentiment analysis of movie reviews. https://rpubs.com/cen0te/naivebayes-sentimentpolarity.

Keller, B. (2003). God and George W. Bush. *New York Times* May 17. www.nytimes.com/2003/05/17/opinion/god-and-george-w-bush.html (accessed August 16, 2020).

Kohn, R. H. (1972). The Washington administration's decision to crush the Whiskey Rebellion. *The Journal of American History*, *59*(3), 567–584.

Lei, L., & Wen, J. (2019). Is dependency distance experiencing a process of minimization? A diachronic study based on the State of the Union addresses. *Lingua*, S002438411930511X. https://doi.org/10.1016/j .lingua.2019.102762.

Liang, T. P., Li, X., Yang, C. T., & Wang, M. (2015). What in consumer reviews affects the sales of mobile apps: A multifacet sentiment analysis approach. *International Journal of Electronic Commerce*, *20*(2), 236–260.

Liu, B., Hu, M., & Cheng, J. (2005). Opinion observer. In A. Ellis & T. Hagino (eds.), *The 14th international world wide web conference (WWW2005)* (pp. 342–351). Chiba, Japan. https://doi.org/10.1145/1060745.1060797.

Liu, D., & Lei, L. (2018). The appeal to political sentiment: An analysis of Donald Trump's and Hillary Clinton's speech themes and discourse strategies in the 2016 US presidential election. *Discourse, Context & Media*, *25*, 143–152.

Loureiro, S. M. C., Bilro, R. G., & Japutra, A. (2019), The effect of consumer-generated media stimuli on emotions and consumer brand engagement. *Journal of Product & Brand Management*, *29*(3), 387–408.

Lu, X. (2010). Automatic analysis of syntactic complexity in second language writing. *International Journal of Corpus Linguistics*, *15*, 474–496.

Maas, A. L., Daly, R. E., Pham, P. T., Huang, D., Ng, A. Y., & Potts, C. (2011). Learning word vectors for sentiment analysis. In D. Lin, Y. Matsumoto, & R. Mihalcea (eds.), *Proceedings of the 49th annual meeting of the Association for Computational Linguistics: Human language technologies* (pp. 142–150). Portland, Oregon, USA. www.aclweb.org/anthology/P11-1015.

Martin, J. R., & White, P. R. R. (2005). *The language of evaluation: Appraisal in English*, London & New York: Palgrave/Macmillan.

Mäntylä, M., Graziotin, D., & Kuutila, M. (2018). The evolution of sentiment analysis: A review of research topics, venues, and top cited papers. *Computer Science Review*, *27*, 16–32.

Mohammad, S. M., & Turney, P. (2010). Emotions evoked by common words and phrases: Using mechanical Turk to create an emotion lexicon. In D. Inkpen & C. Strapparava (eds.), *Proceedings of the NAACL HLT 2010 workshop on computational approaches to analysis and generation of emotion in text* (pp. 26–34). Los Angeles, CA. www.aclweb.org/anthology/W10-0204.

Mohammad, S. M., & Turney, P. D. (2013). Crowdsourcing a word-emotion association lexicon. *Computational Intelligence*, *29*(3), 436–465.

Mohammad, S. M., Zhu, X., Kiritchenko, S., & Martin, J. (2015). Sentiment, emotion, purpose, and style in electoral tweets. *Information Processing & Management*, *51*(4), 480–499. https://doi.org/10.1016/j.ipm.2014.09.003.

Mukhtar, N., Khan, M. A., & Chiragh, N. (2018). Lexicon-based approach outperforms supervised machine Learning approach for Urdu sentiment analysis in multiple domains. *Telematics and Informatics*, *35*(8), 2173–2183.

Murthy, D. (2015). Twitter and elections: Are tweets, predictive, reactive, or a form of buzz? *Information, Communication & Society, 18*, 816–831.

Nasukawa, T., & Yi, J. (2003). Sentiment analysis: Capturing favorability using natural language processing. In B. Porter & J. Gennari (eds.), *Proceedings of the 2nd international conference on knowledge capture*, (pp. 70–77). Florida, USA.

Nielsen, F. Å. (2011). A new ANEW: Evaluation of a word list for sentiment analysis in microblogs. In M. Rowe, M. Stankovic, A. Dadzie, & M. Hardey (eds.), *Proceedings of the ESWC2011 Workshop on "Making Sense of Microposts": Big things come in small packages.* (pp. 93–98). Heraklion, Crete, Greece. https://arxiv.org/pdf/1103.2903.

Oscar N, Fox, P. A., Croucher, R., Wernick, R., Keune, J., & Hooker, K. (2017). Machine learning, sentiment analysis, and tweets: An examination of Alzheimer's disease stigma on Twitter. *Journal of Gerontology Series B: Psychological Science Social Science, 72*(5), 742–751.

Pagolu, V. S., Reddy, K. N., Panda G. & Majhi, B. (2016). Sentiment analysis of Twitter data for predicting stock market movements. *International conference on Signal Processing, Communication, Power and Embedded System (SCOPES)* (pp.1345–1350). Paralakhemundi, India.

Pang, B., Lee, L., & Vaithyanathan, S. (2002). Thumbs up? Sentiment classification using machine learning techniques. In *Proceedings of the ACL-02 conference on empirical methods in natural language processing* (pp. 79–86). Stroudsburg, PA.

Parkhe, V. & Biswas, B. (2016). Sentiment analysis of movie reviews: Finding most important movie aspects using driving factors. *Soft Computing, 20*, 3373–3379.

Rambocas, M. & Pacheco, B. G. (2018). Online sentiment analysis in marketing research: A review. *Journal of Research in Interactive Marketing, 12*(2), 146–163.

Ramteke, J., Shah, S., Godhia, D., & Shaikh, A. (2016). Election result prediction using Twitter sentiment analysis. In *Proceedings of the 2016 international conference on inventive computation technologies; ICICT'16* (pp. 1–5). Coimbatore, India. https://doi.org/10.1109/INVENTIVE.2016.7823280.

Ren, F., & Quan, C. (2012). Linguistic-based emotion analysis and recognition for measuring consumer satisfaction: an application of affective computing. *Information Technology and Management, 13*(4), 321–332.

Rinker, T. (2018). *Sentimentr* (Version 2.6.1) [Computer software]. http://github.com/trinker/sentimentr.

Rout, J. K., Choo, K.-K. R., Dash, A. K., Bakshi, S., Jena, S. K., & Williams, K. L. (2018). A model for sentiment and emotion analysis of unstructured social media text. *Electronic Commerce Research, 18*(1), 181–199.

Savoy, J. (2015). Text clustering: An application with the State of the Union addresses. *Journal of the Association for Information Science and Technology, 66*(8), 1645–1654.

Seabrook, E. M., Kern, M. L., Fulcher, B. D., & Rickard, N. S. (2018). Predicting depression from language-based emotion dynamics: Longitudinal analysis of Facebook and Twitter status updates. *Journal of Medical Internet Research, 20*(5), e168. https://doi.org/10.2196/jmir.9267.

Shalev-Shwartz, S. & Ben-David, D. (2014). *Understanding machine learning.* Cambridge: Cambridge University Press.

Shogan, C. J. (2016). The president's State of the Union address: Tradition, function, and policy implications (updated version). *Congressional Research Service, R40132.* https://crsreports.congress.gov/product/pdf/R/R40132 (last assessed August 14, 2020).

Sinclair, J. (1991) *Corpus Concordance Collocation.* Oxford: Oxford University Press.

Sinclair, J. (2004) *Trust the Text: Language, Corpus and Discourse.* London: Routledge.

Singh, V. K., Piryani, R., Uddin, A., & Waila, P. (2013). Sentiment analysis of movie reviews: A new feature-based heuristic for aspect-level sentiment classification. *International mutli-conference on automation, computing, communication, control and compressed sensing (iMac4s), Kottayam* (pp. 712–717). Kottayam, Kerala, India. https://doi.org/10.1109/iMac4s.2013.6526500.

Sonnier, G.P., McAlister, L. & Rutz, O.J. (2011). A dynamic model of the effect of online communications on firm sales. *Marketing Science, 30*(4), pp. 702–716.

Strapparava, C., & Valitutti, A. (2004). WordNet Affect: An affective extension of WordNet. In *Proceedings of the fourth international conference on language resources and evaluation (LREC'04).* European Language Resources Association (ELRA). www.lrec-conf.org/proceedings/lrec2004/pdf/369.pdf.

Taboada, M., Brooke, J., Tofiloski, M., Voll, K., & Stede, M. (2011). Lexicon-based methods for sentiment analysis. *Computational Linguistics, 37*(2), 267–307.

Tausczik, Y. R., & Pennebaker, J. W. (2010). The psychological meaning of words: LIWC and computerized text analysis methods. *Journal of Language and Social Psychology, 29*, 24–54.

Thet, T. T., Na, J., & Khoo, C.S.G. (2010). Aspect-based sentiment analysis of movie reviews on discussion boards. *Journal of Information Science, 36*(6), 823–848.

Tumasjan, A., Sprenger, T. O., Sandner, P. G., & Welpe, I. W. (2011). Election forecasts with Twitter: How 140 characters reflect the political landscape. *Social Science Computer Review, 29*(4), 402–418.

Turney, P. (2002). Thumbs up or thumbs down? Semantic orientation applied to unsupervised classication of reviews. In P. Isabelle, E. Charniak, & D. Lin (eds.), *Proceedings of the 40th Annual Meeting of the Association for Computational Linguistics* (pp. 417–424), Philadelphia, PA.

Unankard, S., Li, X., Sharaf, M., Zhong, J., & Li, X. (2014). Predicting elections from social networks based on sub-event detection and sentiment analysis. In B. Benatallah, A. Bestavros, Y. Manolopoulos, A. Vakali, & Y. Zhang (eds.), *Web information systems engineering – WISE 2014: 15th international conference, proceedings, Part II* (pp. 1–16). Thessaloniki, Greece & Switzerland: Springer International Publishing.

Vinkers, C. H., Tijdink, J. K., & Otte, W. M. (2015). Use of positive and negative words in scientific PubMed abstracts between 1974 and 2014: Retrospective analysis. *BMJ*, h6467. https://doi.org/10.1136/bmj.h6467.

Wang, L., Liu, H., & Zhou, T. (2020). A sequential emotion approach for diagnosing mental disorder on social media. *Applied Sciences, 10*(5), 1–191-19.

Weidmann, N. B., Otto, S., & Kawerau, L. (2018). The use of positive words in political science language. *PS-Political Science and Politics, 51*(3), 625–628.

Weissman, G. E., Ungar, L. H., Harhay, M. O., Courtright, K. R., & Halpern, S. D. (2019). Construct validity of six sentiment analysis methods in the text of encounter notes of patients with critical illness. *Journal of Biomedical Informatics, 89*, 114–121.

Wilks, Y. (2010). Corpus linguistics and computational linguistics. *International Journal of Corpus Linguistics, 15*(3), 408–411.

Wilson, T. Wilder J, & Hoffmann, p. (2005). Recognizing contextual polarity in phrase-level sentiment analysis. In R. Mooney, C. Brew, L. Chien, & K. Kirchhoff (eds.), *Proceedings of human language technology conference and conference on empirical methods in natural language processing* (pp. 347–354). Vancouver, Canada.

Yekrangi, M. & Abdolvand, N. (2020). Financial markets sentiment analysis: developing a specialized lexicon. *Journal of Intelligent Information Systems.* https://doi.org/10.1007/s10844-020-00630-9.

Yuan, B. (2017). *Sentiment analytics: Lexicons construction and analysis.* Unpublished thesis, University of Missouri of Science and Technology. https://scholarsmine.mst.edu/cgi/viewcontent.cgi?article=8668&context=masters_theses.

Zhang, H., Gan, W., & Jiang. B. (2014). Machine learning and lexicon based methods for sentiment classification: A survey. In L. O'Conner (ed.), *Proceedings of 11th Web information system and application conference* (pp. 262–265), Tianjin, China.

Zunic, A, Corcoran, P., & Spasic, I. (2020). Sentiment analysis in health and well-being: Systematic review. *JMIR Medical Informatics*, *8*(1): e16023. https://doi.org/10.2196/16023.

Cambridge Elements ☰

Corpus Linguistics

Susan Hunston
University of Birmingham
Professor of English Language at the University of Birmingham, UK. She has been involved in Corpus Linguistics for many years and has written extensively on corpora, discourse, and the lexis-grammar interface. She is probably best known as the author of *Corpora in Applied Linguistics* (2002, Cambridge University Press). Susan is currently co-editor, with Carol Chapelle, of the Cambridge Applied Linguistics series.

Advisory Board
Professor Paul Baker, *Lancaster University*
Professor Jesse Egbert, *Northern Arizona University*
Professor Gaetanelle Gilquin, *Université Catholique de Louvain*

About the Series
Corpus Linguistics has grown to become part of the mainstream of Linguistics and Applied Linguistics, as well as being used as an adjunct to other forms of discourse analysis in a variety of fields. It continues to become increasingly complex, both in terms of the methods it uses and in relation to the theoretical concepts it engages with. The Cambridge Elements in Corpus Linguistics series has been designed to meet the needs of both students and researchers who need to keep up with this changing field. The series includes introductions to the main topic areas by experts in the field as well as accounts of the latest ideas and developments by leading researchers.

Cambridge Elements ᐀

Corpus Linguistics

Elements in the Series

Multimodal News Analysis across Cultures
Helen Caple, Changpeng Huan and Monika Bednarek

Doing Linguistics with a Corpus: Methodological Considerations for the Everyday User
Jesse Egbert, Tove Larsson and Douglas Biber

Citations in Interdisciplinary Research Articles
Natalia Muguiro

Conducting Sentiment Analysis
Lei Lei and Dilin Liu

Printed in the United States
by Baker & Taylor Publisher Services